understanding **rationalism**

Understanding Movements in Modern Thought
Series Editor: Jack Reynolds

This series provides short, accessible and lively introductions to the major schools, movements and traditions in philosophy and the history of ideas since the beginning of the Enlightenment. All books in the series are written for undergraduates meeting the subject for the first time.

Published

Understanding Empiricism
Robert G. Meyers

Understanding Existentialism
Jack Reynolds

Understanding German Idealism
Will Dudley

Understanding Hegelianism
Robert Sinnerbrink

Understanding Hermeneutics
Lawrence K. Schmidt

Understanding Phenomenology
David R. Cerbone

Understanding Poststructuralism
James Williams

Understanding Rationalism
Charlie Huenemann

Understanding Utilitarianism
Tim Mulgan

Understanding Virtue Ethics
Stan van Hooft

Forthcoming titles include

Understanding Ethics
Tim Chappell

Understanding Environmental Philosophy
Andrew Brennan and Y. S. Lo

Understanding Feminism
Peta Bowden and Jane Mummery

Understanding Naturalism
Jack Ritchie

Understanding Postcolonialism
Jane Hiddleston

Understanding Pragmatism
Axel Mueller

Understanding Psychoanalysis
Matthew Sharpe and
Joanne Faulkner

Understanding Relativism
Howard Sankey

understanding **rationalism**

Charlie Huenemann

ACUMEN

© Charlie Huenemann, 2008

This book is copyright under the Berne Convention.
No reproduction without permission.
All rights reserved.

First published in 2008 by Acumen

Acumen Publishing Limited
Stocksfield Hall
Stocksfield
NE43 7TN
www.acumenpublishing.co.uk

ISBN: 978-1-84465-112-2 (hardcover)
ISBN: 978-1-84465-113-9 (paperback)

British Library Cataloguing-in-Publication Data
A catalogue record for this book is available from the British Library.

Typeset by Graphicraft Limited, Hong Kong.
Printed and bound by Cromwell Press, Trowbridge.

Contents

	Abbreviations	vii
	Acknowledgements	ix
	Introduction	1
1	Descartes's dualistic world	17
2	Descartes's morals and *The Passions of the Soul*	41
3	Spinoza's one substance	61
4	Spinoza's ethics, politics and religion	85
5	Leibniz's world of monads	107
6	Leibniz's justice and freedom	129
	Conclusion	147
	Questions for discussion and revision	155
	Further reading	159
	Bibliography	161
	Index	165

Abbreviations

Full bibliographical details are given in the Bibliography.

AT	René Descartes, *Oeuvres de Descartes*. Numbers refer to volume and page (e.g. AT VII, 72).
DM	G. W. Leibniz, *Discourse on Metaphysics*, in *Philosophical Essays*.
E	B. Spinoza, *Ethics*, in *The Collected Works of Spinoza*. Numbers refer to parts, definitions and axioms, propositions and corollaries (e.g. Ep20s).
M	G. W. Leibniz, *Monadology*, in *Philosophical Essays*.
NEHU	G. W. Leibniz, *New Essays on Human Understanding*.
PW	G. W. Leibniz, *Political Writings*.
TEI	B. Spinoza, *Treatise on the Emendation of the Intellect*, in *The Collected Works of Spinoza*.
UOT	G. W. Leibniz, *On the Ultimate Origination of Things*, in *Philosophical Essays*.

Acknowledgements

I wish to thank several students who read parts of this manuscript and offered their expert opinion as to its intelligibility: Adrianne McBride, Suzy Rashid, Tia Scoffield, Joshua Smith and Justin Whitesides. I would also like to thank Michael Della Rocca, Jack Reynolds and an anonymous reader for extremely helpful suggestions and corrections. I thank Tristan Palmer at Acumen for being a very encouraging and supportive editor.

Introduction

> For thought and being are the same.
>
> (Parmenides 515 BCE)

"Rationalism", like "socialism" and "impressionism", is a very general term. Broadly speaking, it is the view that the innermost skeleton of the universe and the innermost skeleton of the human mind are one and the same. Reason – the "*ratio*" in rationalism – describes both what can exist and what can be thought. Several interesting consequences would follow from this view, if it were true. First, it would follow that if something is conceivable, then it is genuinely possible; and, similarly, if it is inconceivable, then it is impossible. Second, it would follow that nothing in the universe is (at least in principle) beyond our knowledge. And, third, it would follow that when the human mind discerns a logical relation between two ideas, the world must also exhibit a similar relation between the things corresponding to those ideas. In short, rationalism holds that the human mind holds within itself the key for understanding the structure of ultimate reality. For the deepest knowledge of reality, it is sufficient to look within.

In the past, rationalism was usually contrasted with "empiricism", or the view that experience is the key to gaining knowledge of reality. That contrast has proven to be unreliable and misleading. It is not as if there was a group of card-carrying rationalists, who thought reason is everything and experience is nothing, facing off against a group of card-carrying empiricists, who believed just the opposite. Reason and experience are both important to any plausible philosophy. Still, for many years, Descartes, Spinoza and Leibniz were all listed as players on the rationalist team, and Locke, Berkeley and Hume were listed as players on the empiricist team, and harried teachers of philosophy bent and twisted and warped the texts to try to justify the prevailing view that there really was an out-and-out contest between the two teams. Luckily (thanks to several insightful works by a new generation of historians) we are all past that now, and we realize that the various differences among all of these six great philosophers (and several others from the period) are subtle and often surprising. Together they constitute many different teams, fighting many different battles. It turns out that Descartes and Locke share many opinions, as do Berkeley and Leibniz and (on some matters) Hume and Spinoza. Each is unique in several important respects, and any two of them have significant disagreements.

So now that we have overcome that bad old rationalist versus empiricist distinction, it may be possible once again to make use of the general term "rationalism". But now, instead of using it to name an exclusive club, we should use it to name a constellation of philosophical attitudes or doctrines, bearing in mind that there may not be a decisive "litmus test" for determining whether a given philosopher is or is not a rationalist. Perhaps all or most philosophers are rationalists to a degree, or in a certain respect, or on a particular matter. Perhaps some philosophers are rationalist in one way, and not in another. In this introduction I shall try to explain what I take to be this constellation of rationalist attitudes and doctrines. It will be clear that, given this understanding of the term, Descartes, Spinoza and Leibniz are all rationalists *par excellence*. Perhaps they have empiricist leanings as well, in some respects, on certain matters. Perhaps other philosophers should also count as rationalists. All that is fine. The fact remains that these three great philosophers can be profitably grouped together as sharing several important philosophical doctrines, and these doctrines are well worth exploring if we want to get to grips with rationalism.

In this introduction I shall examine those doctrines under two headings, "Rationalist epistemology" and "Rationalist metaphysics". I shall then turn to similarities and differences in the moral, political and religious thoughts of Descartes, Spinoza and Leibniz. Here we will find more differences than similarities.

Rationalist epistemology

Some of the similarities we find among the rationalists have to do with the ways in which they account for human *knowledge*. Perhaps the best way to begin is by setting aside a tempting misconception about rationalist epistemology.

Some people are tempted to think of rationalists as "armchair philosophers" – that is, as philosophers who think that they can understand everything simply by using their own latent powers of imagination. But following this temptation leads to a ridiculous view of rationalism, which might be expressed as follows:

> According to the rationalists, human reason can tell us everything we want to know about reality. So, if we want to know about the world, we simply need to sit in comfortable armchairs and speculate about what seems to us to make the most sense. Whatever we come up with will match how the world is. If others ask how we can be so sure of this, we will tell them that our reason is given to us by God, and all of our ideas are implanted in our minds by God, and God is perfectly good, so God will never allow us to make any intellectual mistakes.

This is a view no thinking person has ever held (or let us so hope). While there are some elements in this view that do in fact link up with important fixtures in rationalist epistemology, the rationalists' views are much more sophisticated and plausible than this silly account would suggest.

It is true that rationalists prize reason, but wrong to go so far as to say that rationalists think reason can tell us everything we want to know. Reason, according to the rationalists, tells us about only some of reality's deepest features. Consider, for example, the following claims:

1. A thing cannot both exist and fail to exist at the same time.
2. Two things equal to a third are equal to each another.
3. Each thing is identical with itself.

These are broad claims made about things in general, and they are claims we know to be true. But *how* do we know they are true? It sounds too weak to say that we know them through experience. Consider someone saying, "I have seen many things, but I've never seen something both existing and not existing," or saying, "All the experiments conducted so far have shown that two things equal to a third are equal to each other." These claims are not the sorts of claims we try to prove through experience. They are, instead, simply *logical*. They are known "through themselves", as some philosophers say. It is not just that we cannot imagine them being false; no one *possibly* could, not even God.

Rationalists maintain that there are some claims whose justification (that is, whose proof) does not rely upon experience, but relies instead upon reason. Note that this does not mean that someone might come to believe these claims without any experience whatsoever. Presumably, you have to know a language, and have some degree of intellectual sophistication, before you can even understand what these claims mean. But once you understand what they mean, your knowledge of them as truths does not depend upon any particular set of experiences you have had. If someone were to say "I know these claims are true because my teacher told me so," or "I know they are true because I have conducted many experiments and have never seen any exceptions to them," we would suspect that they were either playing a joke on us or did not really understand what the claims are saying.

Or this, at any rate, is one thing a rationalist believes: the justification of some important claims is independent of any particular experience. The technical way of saying this is to say that such claims are *"a priori"*. Descartes, Spinoza and Leibniz all believed that there are important *a priori* truths. Moreover, they all agreed on several of the interesting claims that are *a priori* – the claim that God exists, the claim that everything has a cause, and all the claims of mathematics.

How is it possible that we have so much *a priori* knowledge? Here there are interesting differences among the rationalists, but they all agree that it is ultimately due to two things. First, we have in our minds certain concepts or claims that are *innate* (meaning: we are born with them). These concepts or claims are within our minds just in virtue of the fact that our minds are minds; there cannot be a mind lacking these innate features. Second, our minds are endowed with some sort of processing machinery that is capable of deriving sound results from sound input. Let us briefly examine each of these items.

First, innate ideas. In his *Essay concerning Human Understanding* (1690), John Locke launched several criticisms against the doctrine of innate ideas. He pointed out that if claims like "God exists" and "$2 + 2 = 4$" were innate, then we would expect to find that all humans – English and Indian, infant and adult, healthy and disabled – would agree with them. But of course we do not find this to be true. Furthermore, if all of mathematics is innate, then why do so many of us find the subject so difficult? And, finally, can we really expect that a human newborn, crying out for milk and warmth, is at the same time thinking of triangles, and necessary beings, and the fact that things equal to a third are equal to each other? This all seems preposterous. But, as Leibniz argued in his *New Essays on Human Understanding* (written in 1704), Locke had misunderstood the doctrine of innate ideas. The doctrine does not say that innate ideas should be obvious to all people in all circumstances, nor that no experience is required to come to be aware of innate ideas. Instead, identifying an idea or claim as innate is only to claim that a mind is, by its nature, inclined towards recognizing such an idea or claim as valid. Leibniz offered an analogy:

> If the soul were like a blank slate [as Locke suggested] then truths would be in us as the shape of Hercules is in a piece of marble when the marble is entirely neutral as to whether it assumes this shape or some other. However, if there were veins in the block which marked out the shape of Hercules rather than other shapes, then that block would be more determined to that shape and Hercules would be innate in it, in a way, even though labor would be required to expose the veins and to polish them into clarity, removing everything that prevents them from being seen. This is how ideas and truths are innate in us – as inclinations, dispositions, tendencies, or natural potentialities... (NEHU: 52)

So, following Leibniz's analogy, we can say that while everyone has a certain stock of ideas or truths within them, not everyone has gone through the experience of having those ideas "exposed" and "polished into clarity". In order for that to happen, one must devote a great deal of attention to the matter, thinking hard and working through logical demonstrations in order to get a sharp and clear sense of the ideas and truths we are born with. What this means is that calling these ideas and truths "innate" does not point to their obviousness so much as to the depth or centrality they have in our minds.

Still, Locke would press, why say that we are *born with* these ideas and truths, instead of simply concluding that we eventually see them through the exercise of thinking and demonstrating? Why say the shape of Hercules was *hidden* in the marble, instead of saying that the sculptor *brought* that shape to the marble? In reply, Leibniz would ask what it really means to say that the exercise of our reason leads us to see these ideas and truths. Is this not just to say that our minds incline towards seeing them? And how are we to explain this inclination without positing some structure that is innate to the mind?

Let us now turn our attention from innate ideas to the doctrine that our minds possess some kind of special processing machinery. Each rationalist discovered a set of innate ideas or truths and then deduced consequences from them. The process of deduction is just what we know as reasoning, or logic. When, from guaranteed premises, a conclusion is soundly derived, we can have as much confidence in the conclusion as we did in the premises. Spinoza's *Ethics* is a great display of this. Each part of the *Ethics* begins with definitions and axioms, and then there follows a host of propositions that are meant to be derived from them. So long as the demonstrations are sound, the propositions should be rendered just as necessary, just as *a priori*, as any of the axioms and definitions.

Such demonstrations and arguments are of central importance to the rationalists. Of course, it is not as if logical arguments are not important to other philosophers. And it is not as if the rationalists have no interest in what can be learned through experience and experiments. But when it comes to discerning and describing the deepest fixtures of reality – how the world *must* be – rationalists have the strongest confidence in the power of logical demonstration. At some times, this led rationalists such as Spinoza to confuse causal relations (that hold, say, between a spark and an explosion) with logical relations (that hold between a premise and a conclusion). Two things may be causally related even if their ideas have no logical relation to one another (a lesson driven home to us by David Hume). But rationalists, at times, think the world must run according to the very same logic, the very same rules, that govern our thoughts.

Recognizing the importance of logic to rationalism leads us to a further distinction that rationalists typically draw. The distinction is between the *intellect* and the *imagination*. The general hallmarks of the distinction are that the intellect is logical, while the imagination is psychological; the conclusions of the intellect are valid for all, while the conclusions of the imagination vary from individual to individual; the intellect does not make mistakes about reality, while the imagination can. A vivid way of drawing this distinction can be found in Descartes's sixth meditation, where he considers a thousand-sided figure:

> If I want to think of a chiliagon, although I understand that it is a figure of a thousand sides just as well as I understand the triangle to be a three-sided figure, I do not in the same way imagine the thousand sides or see them as if they were present before me ... [My representation of it] differs in no way from the representation I should form if I were thinking of a myriagon, or any figure with very many sides. Moreover, such a representation is useless for recognizing the properties which distinguish a chiliagon from other polygons ... Imagination

requires a peculiar effort of mind which is not required for understanding; this additional effort of mind clearly shows the difference between imagination and pure understanding.

(AT VII, 72)

It is hard to make a mental image of a chiliagon. But this difficulty does not stop us from understanding and inferring many things about such a figure. For example, do we not know that the sum of the angles of a chiliagon would be greater than the sum of the angles of a triangle? Indeed, we can even work out exactly what the sum of the angles of a regular chiliagon is, despite the fact that we cannot clearly imagine the figure. (As will be seen again in Chapter 1: just draw lines from the centre to each corner, and make a thousand triangles; then multiply that one thousand by 180 degrees; and, finally, subtract 360 degrees from the total so as to remove the angles at the centre of the chiliagon. The result is 179,640 degrees.) We can reach this conclusion with perfect confidence, even when we cannot picture a chiliagon to ourselves. Furthermore, we know this conclusion is correct no matter how individuals might differ in their cloudy and inadequate mental pictures of chiliagons and triangles. The power of logic – at least in this matter – supersedes the power of imagining.

Descartes goes on to account for this difference by linking up the imagination with the body, and linking up the intellect with the pure mind or soul. The brain has some way of encoding the objects of the imagination. Descartes thought it had to do with physical impressions on the brain tissue, while today we would give some account of neurons and electrical states. Either way, our physiological capacities to imagine things are liable to all sorts of problems, ranging from built-in limitations of the organ to strokes, injuries and the ingestion of contraband substances. The pure mind, according to Descartes, is free from these sorts of limitations, and can reach its conclusions without worrying about being compromised by the body's infirmities. And although it is harder to see exactly how either Spinoza or Leibniz is able to provide equivalent freedom for the intellect in their philosophies, each of them manages to find some way to trust in the intellect's capacity to get things right, even when the body is poised to get things wrong.

So far we have seen three epistemological similarities among the rationalists: (1) the belief in *a priori* truths; (2) the belief in the innateness of at least some ideas or truths; and (3) the belief in privileged cognitive machinery (logical processes) in human beings, which allows for a distinction between the intellect and the imagination. To these we should add one more general feature of the epistemological perspective of rationalism: a certain variety of otherworldliness. As we also find in Plato (c. 428–347 BCE), the rationalists place what reason tells them above what the senses reveal. The body and its sense organs can be fooled, and human experience is so limited and prejudiced that it is unreliable as a witness. But reason is a kind of oracle, a way in which we can witness what is true. The way is often difficult and complicated, to be sure, but there is a promise of discovering the innermost nature of things, even when the surfaces suggest something very different. The rationalists trust reason, and not experience, to reveal *what truly is*. And so the rationalists often seem otherworldly, in the sense that the world they take as the true world is not the world revealed by our eyes, ears and fingertips, but a world described through abstract concepts and mathematics.

This deep attitude is expressed in what Plato has Socrates say, as he faces his own death in the *Phaedo*:

> The body keeps us busy in a thousand ways because of its need for nurture. Moreover, if certain diseases befall it, they impede our search for the truth . . . If we are ever to have pure knowledge, we must escape from the body and observe matters in themselves with the soul by itself. (*Phaedo*: 66b–e)

Though each of the rationalists may have had some reservations about this talk of escaping the body, it is true that they all shared the spirit behind the remarks. Knowledge of the deepest truths requires us to transcend our sense experience and embrace reason's own conclusions.

Rationalist metaphysics

Epistemology concerns how we know what is real; metaphysics concerns what is real. It is hard not to allow the views about one influence views about the other. And so just as there are epistemological similarities among the rationalists, we also find metaphysical similarities.

First, there is the otherworldliness just mentioned. Just as the rationalists place more trust in reason than in the senses, they also take the world revealed by reason to be *more real* than the world revealed by the senses. This can be seen in the overall argument Descartes presents in his *Meditations on First Philosophy*. As we shall see, Descartes tries to doubt everything he can in order to discover what he is truly certain of. He finds it easy to doubt his senses, and harder to doubt what his intellect tells him. Eventually he manages to restore his trust in his intellect – by proving the existence of a benevolent creator – and only later does he manage to restore some (but not complete) trust in what his senses reveal. This was his way of helping to usher in a new mathematical physics: for, by the end of his *Meditations*, our science of nature will be based on the concepts and principles of the intellect (which give us mathematics), and not our sensory observations. Descartes, like Galileo, believed that the book of nature is written in the language of mathematics. Mathematics reveals the true world; our senses give us only an approximation of that reality.

This notion that the world discovered by reason is *more real* than the one revealed by the senses introduces a second metaphysical similarity found among the rationalists. Descartes, Spinoza and Leibniz believed in a thesis we can call "the gradations of reality" thesis:

Things can have varying degrees of reality.

This thesis will no doubt sound very weird to us, as we usually take reality to be an all-or-nothing affair: a thing is real, or it is not. But then again, do we really believe this? A rainbow, for example, is something we take to be real, since we can point it out to others and marvel at its beauty. But it is not *as real* as the light and water droplets that allow the rainbow to appear. We cannot actually touch a rainbow, or get to the end of it, since it is like a mirage or illusion. But we can get to the water droplets and seize them, or fly into the sky and block the rays of light, if we want to. So is a rainbow real? Yes, we should say, though not *as real* as the conditions that produce it. We might make similar observations about an economic recession, or a cloud (or indeed about "rationalism" itself): these are things that have some degree of reality, though they are not as real as the processes, entities or individual beliefs that in some way give rise to them.

Descartes finds that his ideas of stones, men, angels and God are ideas whose objects have varying degrees of reality. God is the "most real" of all his ideas, and his ideas of other things always seem to be lacking something or other – perhaps they lack information about their causes, or how they came about. Spinoza thinks that substances are more real if they have more attributes. Leibniz thinks the spatiotemporal world is less real than the substances that give rise to it. They each hold the gradations of reality thesis. What is more, they all also maintain that the degree of a thing's reality is proportional to the degree of its *perfection*. Again, we usually think of "perfection" as all or nothing;

calling one thing "more perfect" than another sounds wrong. But at least in the seventeenth century, "perfection" meant something more along the lines of *completeness*. Things can be complete in varying degrees: one house can be more complete ("more finished"?) than another. Similarly, according to the rationalists, beings can be more complete than others. God represents the greatest degree of completeness, of perfection, of reality. *Nothing* – meaning the void – is completely incomplete, imperfect, unreal. Everything else falls in between. Humans have some perfection and some reality. Angels, perhaps, a bit more. Animals, a bit less.

One way to think of the matter is as follows. Let us suppose that ultimately there is a finite number of genuine properties (or "perfections") any individual thing can have. Stacking the deck just a little, let us suppose that these qualities are power, knowledge and goodness. Let there be one being who possesses all possible perfections in the highest possible degree (and call that being "God"). Then there may be some beings with lesser power, lesser knowledge and lesser goodness. Each of these beings is less real and less perfect than God. And there may be beings with even less power, knowledge and goodness; these beings are less real and perfect than the previous beings. And so on. If we imagine three knobs marked "power", "knowledge" and "goodness", then we can imagine each being as what we get when those knobs are turned to various possible positions.

In the chapters of this text we shall find this notion doing a lot of metaphysical work (and, in the case of Leibniz, moral work as well). The chapters will provide further explanations of the gradations of reality thesis, as employed in those different contexts. What should be most striking to us overall is just how obvious these rationalists take this thesis to be. Nowhere do they offer a careful explication of it, let alone a defence for it. They took it to be perfectly obvious – and apparently, to many of their immediate readers, it was.

Perhaps it is obvious by now that all of these rationalists believed in God. Descartes and Leibniz believed in the God of Christianity. Spinoza believed in an entity he thought could be called either "God" or "Nature" (in Latin, *Deus sive Natura*), but this entity is more of an impersonal force, and not the sort of deity to pray to or to worship. Believing in some sort of supreme being may be an irresistible consequence of believing in the gradations of reality thesis; for once we allow that reality comes in degrees, is it not hard to resist the conclusion that there is some being with maximal reality? But belief in a supreme being also can provide a sort of foundation for rationalist epistemology as well. We see this most explicitly in one of Leibniz's arguments for God's existence. In the *Monadology*, Leibniz argues that if there are indeed *a priori* concepts, then there must be some sort of foundation for their existence. In other words, there must be some real being whose existence gives those concepts some sort of reality. It cannot be any finite mind, since presumably the *a priori* truths based on those concepts would not cease being true if all of the finite minds died, disintegrated or vanished. It must be an infinite mind – that is, God. "God's understanding is the realm of eternal truths or of the ideas on which they depend; without him there would be nothing real in possibles, and not only would nothing exist, but also nothing would be possible" (M: §43). This notion of God reveals what a rationalist really wants from God, at least in so far as the rationalist is doing philosophy: God is the ultimate library of concepts and essences, an eternal storehouse of all the *a priori* ideas we will need to employ in framing our metaphysics of the world. By placing concepts in God's mind for safe storage, so to speak, we escape the danger of any kind of historical or psychological relativism. That is to say, the concepts we are playing with are not just those that our historical age has managed to cook up; they belong to the eternal mind of God.

We have seen that the rationalists find it extremely important to distinguish the intellect from the imagination: the imagination is liable to all sorts of distortions and limitations, whereas the intellect is not. Accompanying this need is the metaphysical belief in a soul. Descartes believed in the existence of the soul in a straightforward way: each human being is a fusion of a material body with an immaterial soul, two separate substances conjoined in some mysterious metaphysical union. Upon the death of the body, the soul may continue to exist, and go to heaven (or whatever). Leibniz also believed that the human mind is immaterial, although (as we shall see) he did not believe that it could exist without being conjoined in some fashion to some physical thing. He thought that our souls are always conjoined to some body or other, until that final day – the day of resurrection – when they are joined to an incorruptible human body for the rest of time. Spinoza carefully demonstrated that the mind and the body are one and the same thing, conceived in two different ways, which certainly makes it sound as if he did not believe that the soul was a thing that could exist separate from the body. But this did not stop him from trying to demonstrate, near the end of the *Ethics*, more than a dozen propositions that concern "the mind's duration without any relation to the body" (5p20s) and it did not stop him from writing that "we feel and know by experience that we are eternal" (5p23s). Although Spinoza certainly did not offer any sort of Christian afterlife of the kind dreamt of by Descartes and Leibniz, he did leave room for some kind of rationalist afterlife, one characterized by pure knowledge and the purely intellectual love of God.

We have described four broad metaphysical similarities found within the philosophies of Descartes, Spinoza and Leibniz: (1) the reality of the world revealed by reason; (2) the gradations of reality thesis; (3) the existence of God; and (4) the existence of the soul. Of course, these similarities should not obscure the fact that there are also deep and interesting differences among the metaphysical systems of each of these philosophers. Indeed, once we begin to study the particular features of each philosophy, we are likely to see only the differences.

Morals, politics and religion

We find significant similarities in the epistemology and metaphysics of our three rationalists. But in their morals, politics and religion we find very important differences. In fact, under each topic, we find two of them opposed to the third; and which two are aligned varies with the topic. Let us take each in turn.

Morals

Both Descartes and Spinoza advocate a moral philosophy that is rooted in Stoicism. The Stoics believed that the moral life results from two things: reason's command over the passions, and the recognition that most of life's events are completely beyond our control. The passions, it is thought, typically involve confusions about what is happening to us. Perhaps we feel joy in another person's company, and come to love them, and then become willing to do all sorts of ridiculous or dangerous things for their sake. Or perhaps we are suffering from a headache, and then someone pesters us with a naive question, and we unleash our fury upon them. We can avoid such irrational actions by soberly diagnosing what we are experiencing and devoting our minds to what reason dictates. At the same time, we should recognize that the universe is bigger than we are, infinitely greater in complexity and power. Things will not always go our way, and there is nothing we can do about that. So why be disappointed? Why not accept that much of life is beyond our control, and resign ourselves to what we cannot change or avoid? Observe, detach and remain calm: this is the basic Stoic regimen.

Stoicism does lead an individual to a set of moral precepts or rules, and into a certain kind of life. To the extent that we shall need the comforts and protection of civil society in order to carry out our philosophical meditations, we shall need to be good citizens and take some interest in others' well-being. Note this well: the Stoic needs to be concerned with the state and with fellow citizens only to the extent that such concern will aid the Stoic in living life under reason's dictates. Descartes is especially concerned with keeping society and civil obligations at arm's length. Spinoza, as we shall see, believed in taking on more civil responsibility, but in the end he also leaves open an escape route so that he is always able to retreat into a semi-private world of untroubled reflection. Both philosophers wrote extensively about how to employ reason to govern the passions, and both resigned themselves to the order of nature.

Leibniz, however, does not base his moral thought upon any kind of Stoicism. The central moral notion in his philosophy is *justice*, which he defines as the charity (or love) of the wise. Wise human beings are able to discern the metaphysical perfection in creatures, and are able to judge the extent to which fellow creatures are deserving of love. Leibniz believed that we are obligated to be just, and as our reward we feel a great satisfaction when we manage to act with justice. Unlike that of Descartes and Spinoza, Leibniz's morality asks us to take a genuine interest in others' well-being, for their own sakes, as well as for the sake of the disinterested pleasure we experience in seeing justice done. There is much more to be said about this, but for now the quick summary is that while the moralities of Descartes and Spinoza are fundamentally egoistic ("what's in it for me?"), Leibniz's morality is non-egoistic.

Politics

As was just said, Descartes tries to keep civil obligations at arm's length. In both his early and late moral codes, he recommends adjusting oneself to the demands of the political institutions of the day. If nothing else, staying out of politics is conducive to peace of mind and allows for uninterrupted philosophical meditation. Give Caesar his due, Descartes could be imagined as saying, so that you will be able to carry out your own philosophy without incident. Descartes devoted very little thought to politics or the philosophical foundations of the state.

But Spinoza and Leibniz wrote extensively about politics. Spinoza's *Tractatus Theologico-Politicus* (1671) and his *Tractatus Politicus* (left unfinished at the time of his death) argued that democratic republics are the most stable and optimal form of government. They are the least likely to decay into civil war, since citizens usually do not rebel against governments in which they have a voice. Moreover, he argued that democratic republics are also consistent with granting citizens an extensive set of liberties, especially the liberty to freely publish one's thoughts. In a republic, he thought, there must be nearly complete freedom of speech, since open discussion and argument are the means by which a democracy is run. These political concerns were especially relevant in Spinoza's own historical context, as the Dutch Republic was in the course of reverting to a monarchy. Spinoza argued (unsuccessfully) that this revolution would run counter to the self-interest of the citizens.

Leibniz had deep political concerns as well. Indeed, it seems that he took up the position of "courtly philosopher" in the hopes of coaching monarchs to establish peaceful and just governments. He did not favour democratic republics, but tried to model his vision of earthly monarchs on what he knew about the divine monarch, God, whose decree resulted in the existence of the best of all possible worlds. Mortal monarchs should follow God's lead, Leibniz thought, issuing the decrees that will bring their kingdoms into their best possible forms. As in his morals, justice is the fundamental notion in Leibniz's political philosophy. The just kingdom is the one that ensures that its citizens get what they deserve. In other words, they ensure that the citizens are loved in proportion to the metaphysical perfection they exhibit. This requires that the state use whatever means it has to ensure that its citizens flourish as human beings, in the use of their reason, their wisdom and their goodness. Most of the royalty he advised, however, found personal aggrandizement more attractive than Leibnizian virtue.

Religion

Here we find Descartes and Leibniz opposed to Spinoza. Both Descartes and Leibniz were Christians. Although Descartes was criticized in his own day for creating a philosophy that seemed to run on its own without much help from Christian doctrine, in fact he sought to ensure that each feature of his philosophy would cohere with his own Catholicism. He believed that the existence of God and the distinction between soul and body are demonstrable through reason, and he offered those demonstrations. He also put God to work in several areas of his metaphysics: God is responsible for framing the logical skeleton shared by both the world and the human mind, and responsible as well for the re-creation of the world at every instant in time. He believed that through revelation – a source of knowledge that goes beyond reason's powers – we discover further features of God, such as that God is triune, that Jesus is fully divine and fully human, and so on. His temperament was to try to avoid the various political and doctrinal controversies of the Church, and so he often stayed silent about these matters, but there is no reason to doubt that he was a sincere believer.

Leibniz was even more interested in building Christianity into his philosophy. Like Descartes, he thought that the central dogmas of Christianity are known only through revelation, not reason, but Leibniz worked hard to ensure that the particular claims of Christian dogma could be put into the terms of his own metaphysics. Miracles, transubstantiation, resurrection and other concepts were explained carefully, with utmost attention to detail, in the metaphysics of substances, monads and perceptions. This was perhaps chiefly due to Leibniz's devout Christianity, and to his equally devout mission to forge a thorough and comprehensive metaphysical vision. It was also part of an overall campaign to heal the rupture of the Reformation, and seek a reunion of Catholicism and Protestantism. Such a religious union was required if Leibnizian justice were ever to be seen in Europe, he believed.

Spinoza, in contrast, was seen as atheistic, impious and profoundly anti-Christian. His *Tractatus Theologico-Politicus*, in addition to arguing for democratic republicanism, also argued that the Bible was written by primitive people unacquainted with science and philosophy. As a consequence, what they wrote was infected with illusions, exaggerations and misconceptions. From the Bible we may be able to learn some history, and some features of an ancient people's way of looking at the world, and even some sound moral advice, but we shall not learn anything about the metaphysical features of reality. For that we must turn to philosophy and embrace the consequences of reason. That being said, Spinoza writes, it may be that religion has its political uses. People who are not adept at following reason's dictates may be controlled through the imagery of the Bible (the fear of hell and hope of heaven, especially). But the wise person knows better than to take any of these notions seriously.

So the moral, political and religious thought of these rationalists show considerable disunity. We might summarize the differences as follows:

Question	Descartes	Spinoza	Leibniz
Is morality based on self-interest?	Yes	Yes	No
Does morality entail specific political recommendations?	No	Yes	Yes
Is Christianity true?	Yes	No	Yes

Such a summary does not do justice to the thoughts of these philosophers, of course. But it does indicate that the similarities found in the epistemologies and metaphysics do not translate into similarities in other domains. This may come as some surprise, since one might initially think that philosophers with similar views of reason and reality will have similar things to say about morals, politics and religion. Not so.

one
Descartes's dualistic world

Biography

René Descartes was born in La Haye, France, in 1596. His mother died less than a year later, after giving birth to Descartes's sister, and soon thereafter his father began travelling away on legal and political business for more than six months out of the year. Descartes and his sister and their older brother were left in the care of friends and relatives, and by the time he was ten, Descartes was sent away to a rigorous Jesuit boarding school aimed at turning boys into pious and gracious gentlemen. He was bookish, small, and weak in health. He received a thorough education in classical literature and Latin, and excelled in mathematics. After boarding school he followed family tradition and studied to be a lawyer, and received his law degree by the time he was 20. But by then he realized that he did not want to be a lawyer, and he was not sure what to do with himself.

It was expected that his older brother would inherit his father's title and most of his wealth, and Descartes was not entitled to any share in the family's holdings until he turned 25. So for the next five years Descartes signed up with the military and served in various capacities as a soldier throughout France, Holland and Germany. Not much is known about his activities, although we know that he continued to develop his knowledge of mathematics and physics, and began to form a vision of his own philosophy. He also learned the art of gambling, and – given his skills in mathematics – he was probably pretty good at it.

When he turned 25 he took possession of some family properties and promptly sold them. And again for the next six or seven years little is known about his endeavours. He travelled to Italy, spent most of his time in Paris, made friends, and continued with his studies in mathematics and science – and of course probably did all the things any young man of independent means would do while trying to find his way in the world. He was a disappointment to his father and older brother, who would have preferred Descartes to become serious and establish a more stable and secure mode of life.

By 1628, as he entered his thirties, he was ready to leave the diversions and controversies of Paris and hide himself in rural Holland. He had found his direction. He felt that he had a genuine contribution to make in philosophy, and he needed to be free of distraction in order to make it. It was clear to him that our vision of the world needs to be firmly grounded in the results of science, experiments and mathematics. So he began experimenting, making lenses, practising dissection, and deducing his own conclusions. By 1633 he had bound up his view of the world in a work he aptly entitled *The World*, and was ready to send it to the publishers, when he received startling news: the Catholic Church had condemned Galileo for his belief that the earth revolved around the sun. Descartes had agreed with Galileo, and had said so in *The World*. He certainly did not want to be condemned and (like Galileo) placed under house arrest for the rest of his life, and so he was not sure what to do.

He retreated and regrouped, and reworked *The World* into a set of separate essays on geometry, optics and meteorology, all prefaced with a *Discourse on Method*, published in 1637. This was followed four years later by a work that laid the metaphysical groundwork for his scientific approach to the world, *Meditations on First Philosophy*. He published the *Meditations* with a set of objections from several notable European intellectuals, and his replies to them. This was followed four years later by his four-part *Principles of Philosophy*, a work that explained the entire Cartesian system and was intended by its author to become the standard textbook for philosophy and natural science throughout Europe. It very nearly did.

Descartes held as his motto that "he who is hidden lives well", but his publications brought him into the public spotlight. He was recognized immediately as among the top mathematicians of his time, and people saw him as a fiercely intelligent critic of the established scientific, philosophical and theological orthodoxy – an intellectual rebel. Many saw him as he presented himself: a spokesman for plain sense, crashing through the delicate lattice of scholastic philosophy with the battering ram of the new experimental, mechanical science. (Once, when someone asked to see his library, Descartes showed him a body he was dissecting and said, "This is my library.") And as often as he was attacked, he answered back with matching vehemence and venom – which only inflamed his enemies all the more, of course. He never yielded an inch to his critics and often made it seem as if they simply had not read his works carefully enough. At the very least, his replies to critics are stunning intellectual performances on his part.

We can sense an interesting tension between Descartes's works and his life. His works suggest a solo act, that of a man who is more interested in conquering himself than the world, and a man who wants nothing but some peace in which to carry out his own reasonable meditations on philosophy, mathematics and nature. But his life was filled with friends, enemies, jealousy, pride, fame and controversy. He was father to a daughter, Francine, whom he cherished, and who was taken from him by sickness when she was just five years old. He never married, nor (from what we know) had romantic attachments after that. His last published work was *The Passions of the Soul* (1649), in which he tried to teach how to keep one's health, cheer and tranquillity even when facing the harshest tragedies of life.

He became increasingly entangled in scholarly and religious controversies through the late 1640s, and in 1649 he accepted an invitation to serve as tutor to Christina, the Queen of Sweden. There, in the bitter Nordic winter, he caught pneumonia and died in 1650. He was 54.

Descartes tried to bring about two revolutions in his lifetime. One of them was epistemological: he tried to base his philosophy on simple ideas that his readers could discover for themselves, rather than dogmas that had been handed down through the centuries. The other revolution was in metaphysics: Descartes described the world in terms that fit with the new mechanical, mathematical science of the world ushered in by Galileo. These revolutions also helped to shape his moral and religious philosophy, which we shall examine in Chapter 2.

The *Meditations*

We can begin our examination of Descartes's philosophy by basing it on his *Meditations on First Philosophy* (1641). The *Meditations* is written like a guidebook meant to help any pilgrim blessed with common sense to arrive at the most fundamental philosophical truths. So this also makes it a good introduction to his philosophical system. We shall begin by following its presentation loosely, and then we shall explore various other regions of his philosophical worldview as they present themselves.

First, though, a word about Descartes's style in the *Meditations*. It is not a work in which Descartes simply lays out what he thinks is true. Rather, the work recounts his discoveries as he meditates on his beliefs about the world. It is a chronicle of his discoveries, like an experimental log. There is a lot of give-and-take; Descartes will assert something, then doubt it, think further, and then embrace the conclusion for reasons quite different from those originally given for it. We shall not chronicle this give-and-take (or "dialectic") style of the work, although it is an elegant portrayal of the way in which philosophical reflection takes place.

Doubting

In the *Meditations*, Descartes tries to determine what he really knows. He realizes that he has been taught many things that he has later discovered to be false, and he wants to know whether he can settle once and for all what is true. So, for example, he had been taught that the earth stood still, and the sun went around it; and now he believed (though was not quite willing to proclaim) that the earth revolved around the sun. Is there any way we can sort through all of our beliefs, and get rid of the ones that might be false? In order to begin this project, he looks for what he cannot possibly doubt. But how does one go about finding what is *indubitable*? What is it to doubt something? Is it enough to simply say "I doubt it"? That's too easy. Instead, Descartes suggests that we use the following criterion to determine whether any claim ("X") can be doubted:

> *X can be doubted* = I can conceive some scenario (even one that seems outrageous and bizarre) in which X would be false, but I still would believe that X is true.

The criterion demands that, when we doubt something, we not only imagine some way that the claim we are doubting could be false, but we also explain why we would have come to believe that it were true. So, for example, we can doubt that "Human beings have travelled to the moon" by supposing that no humans ever went there, and by supposing that there has been some vast cover-up (with fake film footage and so on) to make it seem to everyone that humans have walked on the moon. Descartes pushes this strategy to the limit, since he wants to find what cannot *possibly* be doubted. That is, *any* possible scenario counts – even one that no one takes seriously.

Using this criterion, he succeeds in doubting *everything* that our senses have ever told us – everything we have ever seen, heard or read. He does this by suggesting the scenario that our experience has been only a dream. Suppose we are dreaming, and have been dreaming our whole lives; if so, then we cannot trust anything we have seen, heard or felt. All of our experience would be an illusion, cooked up perhaps in our subconscious. Of course, it does not *seem* to us now that we are dreaming; but then again, that is how it is in dreams, isn't it? It never seems to us that we are dreaming, even when the most outlandish things are happening. So the mere *feeling* that we are not dreaming does not prove anything.

But Descartes has not finished yet. He thinks there are some truths that we would still know even if we were dreaming. For our dreams, he observes, are not purely random noise. They are weird, to be sure, but they make some sense. Objects usually move around in the way that we think they do in waking life; there are relations between causes and effects; and the basic geometry and arithmetic of the world remain constant. In short, the dream world is still much like the waking world, in some fundamental ways, even if some strange things are happening in it. Perhaps if we are dreaming we cannot be sure of the particulars of our experience; but even if we are dreaming we can still be sure about these more fundamental features of experience. Or can we?

Descartes manages to doubt these more fundamental features by suggesting that, for all we know, there is some vastly powerful being (like God) who has power over our minds, and who is capable of making certain features and facts appear to be fundamental and true when really they are arbitrary and false. This great deceiver could make it seem obvious to us that unaffected bodies retain their shapes and that $2 + 3 = 5$ when the truth is something much weirder and unimaginable. If we take seriously this scenario of a godlike being intent upon deceiving us, then Descartes argues that we can doubt even those things that seem to us most clearly and distinctly to be true. And at this point, we cannot rule out this scenario; it seems possible after all, though frightening and bizarre (not to mention paranoid).

At this point, Descartes thinks he has reached a limit, and has doubted everything he can. The question, though, is whether anything is left standing. Let us imagine that our experience is entirely at the mercy of some vastly powerful entity, who makes us have experiences that do not match up at all with how the world really is. In that case, is there anything that is wholly *indubitable*?

Cogito

In the second meditation, Descartes finds one such indubitable truth: "I exist." For I can conceive no scenario, no matter how bizarre, in which "I exist" would be false but *I* would still believe it to be true. Descartes is certain of his own existence because any act of thinking or doubting on his part presupposes his own existence, at least as a thinking thing. So long as he is thinking, he knows he exists. Not even God could deceive a nonexistent being into thinking it exists when in fact it does not – for there would be no one to deceive! This insight is often referred to among philosophers as "the cogito", which is shorthand for the Latin sentence *cogito, ergo sum* – "I think, therefore I am."

Is the cogito valid? It may seem to us perfectly obvious that a nonexistent being cannot be deceived about anything – but what guarantees this insight? If God can deceive us about the apparent truth of $2 + 3 = 5$, why could God not also deceive us about the cogito? Descartes can reply that the cogito is genuinely different from the claims that we doubted under the deceiving-God scenario. It simply is not genuinely possible for us to conceive a scenario in which we are deceived into thinking we exist. We can mouth the words "Maybe I really do not exist but I still falsely believe that I do," but it is impossible to take the idea seriously – we keep bumping into ourselves. This is basically what Descartes says in the *Principles of Philosophy*: "For it is a contradiction to suppose that what thinks does not, at the very time when it is thinking, exist" (AT VIIIA, 7). Trying to deny the cogito brings about not exactly a logical contradiction, but a kind of *performative* contradiction, like saying out loud, "I have lost my voice." Saying it *makes* it false. We do not encounter this kind of contradiction when we try to doubt that $2 + 3 = 5$ or that squares have four sides, since we can conceive of being deceived into thinking these claims are true when they are not. But we cannot imagine being deceived into believing the cogito when it is false. (Just try it!) So the cogito, unlike these other claims, escapes from the "God is deceiving me" scenario, and indeed any such scenario. By Descartes's criterion, the cogito is indubitable.

Later, in the third meditation, Descartes claims that the cogito is shown to him by something he calls *the natural light*. "Whatever is revealed to me by the natural light – for example that from the fact that I am doubting it follows that I exist, and so on – cannot in any way be open to doubt" (AT VII, 46). He does not explain exactly what this natural light is, but it seems to be the "light of reason", or what we can be sure of just in virtue of being rational beings. To be rational is to have a special capacity, and this capacity reveals the truths known through the natural light. We might put it this way: if we assume that we do have reason – that we are not completely insane – then we can be sure of certain rational truths, like the cogito and whatever else is shown by the natural light. And if we doubt our own sanity, then we really cannot be sure of anything at all. (This last doubt, that we might be insane, is a doubt Descartes never takes seriously.)

Thus Descartes believes there are some truths that are indubitable and are known just in virtue of our being rational; they are known independently of any particular experience. These truths, Descartes goes on to explain, are based on ideas we are born with, ideas that are *innate*. The most important innate idea, according to Descartes, is the idea of God. This is an idea we should explore at this point.

God

The cogito does not show much; only that I exist. And this "I" that exists, says Descartes in the second meditation, is only a thinking thing; we do not know for sure that it is connected to any kind of body, or even that there is anything else that exists. It could be a disembodied spirit floating in the void, for all we know. The "I" has experience – that is to say, it *seems* to see things, encounter things, perceive things, and think of things – but by the beginning of the third meditation we have no reason for thinking that this experience is *veridical*. In other words, we have no reason for believing that any of these things we think about really exist.

In the third meditation, Descartes argues that we have reason to believe that the "I" is not alone in the void. He argues this by carefully examining the ideas the "I" has, and figuring out whether the "I" itself could be the cause of them all. His hope is that he might come across some idea that the "I" could not have caused by itself, since then he would have good reason for believing that something else exists – namely, the cause of that idea, whatever it is.

This strategy will work only if Descartes knows what it takes for something to be the *cause* of an idea. He thinks he does, and we may call it the *causal adequacy principle*:

The cause of any idea must itself be sufficient for producing everything that is in the content of that idea.

Or, in Descartes's terminology, the cause of any idea must have at least as much *formal reality* as there is *objective reality* in the idea. "Formal reality" is meant to capture just how much causal power the cause of the idea has; "objective reality" is meant to capture the causal powers of the object that is represented in the idea. So the causal powers represented in the idea cannot exceed the causal powers of the thing causing that idea. We cannot have an idea of a fancy, complicated, powerful thing unless it is caused by something that is just as fancy, complicated and powerful. Put much more simply: a lesser thing cannot bring about a greater thing. This principle – which is related to what other philosophers call "the principle of sufficient reason" – is shown by the natural light, according to Descartes. If so, then it is supposed to be as indubitable as the cogito.

Here we may wish to pause and consider whether the causal adequacy principle really is indubitable. Why could something not just appear, for no cause at all? Or why could an idea rich in content not be caused by something very simple? There is no contradiction in supposing these things. Still, for argument's sake, let us suppose it is indubitable, and see how Descartes uses it.

Armed with the causal adequacy principle, Descartes examines the kinds of ideas he has, and asks whether the "I" could have created all of these ideas on its own. But he gets stuck when he considers the idea of God. His idea of God represents a being that is infinite and perfect. But the "I", Descartes argues, does not have sufficient causal powers for generating the content of this idea. The "I" is clearly limited – ignorant, doubtful, and capable of becoming more powerful – whereas God, as represented by our idea of God, is perfect, complete and incapable of becoming greater. Indeed, only God could cause an idea of a thing with this much causal power. Hence, he concludes, God must exist: for only God is sufficient to cause the idea of God.

One plausible objection to this argument Descartes does consider is whether the "I" could generate the idea of God merely by imagining something better than itself, and then something better than that, and so on until forming the abstract idea of a perfect being. Descartes argues that although in fact this may be how we come to learn about God, the very process presupposes that we already have some conception of God buried in our minds. For in order to imagine a chain of beings that grows continuously better, the "I" must already have an idea of what is at the end of that chain – the perfect being who sets the scale. In fact, the idea of God is more basic, says Descartes, than the idea of any finite thing, including our idea of ourselves. The ideas of finite things have the content they have only in virtue of there being the idea of an infinite and perfect being, which can be limited and particularized in various ways so as to generate them. The idea of God thus turns out to be even more fundamental than our idea of ourselves.

One plausible objection Descartes does *not* take seriously enough, however, is whether there really is any content in this idea of God. He claims "it is utterly clear and distinct, and contains in itself more objective reality than any other idea" (AT VII, 46), but then he goes on to admit that it is an idea he does not fully grasp, but can merely touch in his thought. This should be a warning signal that possibly we are not entertaining a genuine idea. Could it be, perhaps, that there is some powerful being deceiving us into thinking that the idea has maximal content when really it has none? Or could it be that we are simply using words "infinite and perfect being" without attaching a genuine idea to them? Could it be that instead of having a genuine idea of God, we simply have a bunch of things we know we are supposed to say about God?

Setting this last objection aside, Descartes intends to use this argument for God's existence in order to remove his most powerful doubt, the doubt that perhaps we are being deceived by some powerful being. If we have a genuine idea of God, and the causal adequacy principle is shown by the natural light, then we may be certain God exists; and furthermore, "it is manifest by the natural light that all fraud and deception depend on some defect" (AT VII, 52), so we may be sure that God is no deceiver. If all this is so – and this is a big *if* – then Descartes no longer has a way to doubt the fundamental features and facts about the world that are present and true even in our dreams. That is to say, the "God is deceiving me" scenario has been ruled out, since God would not deceive us or allow us to be deceived in what we clearly and distinctly perceive.

A rationalist's revolution

We should observe briefly here that rescuing our knowledge of the fundamental features of the world is an important part of the metaphysical revolution Descartes wants to bring about. Other philosophers of the time followed Aristotle's philosophy, and they believed that our science of nature is drawn from sense experience. Their dictum was that there is nothing in the intellect which was not first present to the senses.

Descartes, in the end, champions a very different picture: that we know, independently of experience, the basic mathematical and physical constraints of nature, and this provides the basis for our knowledge of nature. Descartes brings about this revolution in his strategy of doubting: he first finds reasons for doubting what the senses say ("I might be dreaming"), and then he finds reasons to doubt what the intellect understands about the world through mathematics and basic physics ("God might be deceiving me"). He then manages to restore his trust in his intellect ("God exists and is no deceiver") – but it turns out that he never manages to restore quite as much trust in his senses. So, in the end, the intellect has greater authority than the senses, and what we know through the intellect outweighs anything the senses might suggest to us. This is a rationalist's revolution, putting the *intellect* – and not the *senses* – at the foundation of our knowledge.

Intellect

With his first argument for God's existence in the *Meditations*, Descartes has managed to rescue the truths of the intellect from doubt, although he is still able to doubt what the senses tell us. In other words, so far as we know, we may still be dreaming.

But this intellect that Descartes has rescued can tell us many important things about the world, even if we are dreaming. The intellect allows us to construct demonstrations and proofs, as well as recognize claims that are true in virtue of the meanings of the terms. Descartes distinguishes the intellect from the imagination, which is simply our ability to form representations of either real or "merely imagined" objects that are external to us. This imagination is tied to images, or particular sensory experiences; the intellect is not tied down in this way. The intellect considers pure reasons, whether or not we can form images of what we are reasoning about.

There are three important occasions in the meditations when the unique powers of the intellect are called into play, and examining them will help us to understand the role it can play in one's philosophy.

1. In the second meditation, Descartes pauses to consider whether his own existence as a thinking being could really be more certain to him than his knowledge of the bodies that seem to surround him. So he examines a nearby body – a piece of wax – and asks what it is we really know about it. Our senses tell us it is in

constant change: as the wax warms up, it changes in temperature, shape, colour, smell, size and taste. But we know all the while that it is the same hunk of matter undergoing these changes. We know that, in addition to all of the changing sensory qualities, there is *something* that is flexible, malleable and spatial. What tells us about this something? It cannot be the senses, since they inform us only of the changing properties. Descartes's explanation is that the intellect tells us about the nature of extension: our knowledge of the fundamental nature of the wax is understood through the intellect, not gathered through the senses.
2. In the fifth meditation, Descartes writes of a chiliagon, a thousand-sided figure. We cannot form a clear image of a chiliagon, since it is too complicated. But the intellect faces no difficulty in thinking about its properties. For example, if we are considering a regular chiliagon (one that the imagination would portray as roughly circular), the intellect can determine what the sum of its angles must be (as we saw in the introduction). The imagination hence is more limited than the intellect, which is bound only by the range of what is conceptually possible.
3. In the fifth meditation Descartes also offers another argument for God's existence that is based on the power of the intellect. The concept of God is the concept of a being possessing absolutely all perfections. Existence itself is a perfection, in the sense that a being with it has greater power than a being without it. Hence existence belongs in the very concept of God, which is to say that God necessarily exists. This is an argument Descartes could not have provided before the third meditation, since at that time – before he proved that God is not deceiving him – he still was not able to trust his intellect.

The role of the intellect in Descartes's philosophy is one of the key factors in understanding him as a rationalist. The rationalist's credo is that when appearances clash with what the intellect understands, the intellect wins. The intellect is a special pipeline to the truth, and it is not subject to the errors and delusions of the senses, passions and imagination.

Innate ideas

Because of its importance, we should examine the intellect a little further, and discuss the nature of the ideas it comes to know. As has been stated above, Descartes believes that some ideas are *innate*. They belong to our minds just because it would be impossible for a mind to be a mind and lack them; they are required for any kind of thought. For example, it seems impossible for someone to be capable of thought and yet lack the concept of two things being *similar*; in the same way, no thing could think without being able to recognize two things as being *different*. Descartes goes further and claims that to be a thinking being also requires having the idea of God, and of the causal adequacy principle (or its more general version, that a cause must be sufficient for its effect), and of all ideas which the mind is capable of discovering on its own, provided it is attentive and follows logical channels of thought. The intellect is, at least in principle, capable of discovering every idea logic can frame.

In fact, in one of his published works Descartes goes even further and calls *all* ideas innate. He is brought to this conclusion as a result of the way he views the relation between the human mind and the human body. As we shall see later on, Descartes believes that the mind is wholly distinct from the body, and the only effect a body can have upon a mind is to send the mind some sort of signal so that certain innate ideas are "called up" in it. In a short work published in 1648 as an attempt to distance himself from a wayward disciple, Descartes writes that

> there is nothing in our ideas which is not innate to the mind or the faculty of thinking, with the sole exception of those circumstances which relate to experience, such as the fact that we judge that this or that idea which we now have immediately before our mind refers to a certain thing situated outside us. (AT VIIIB, 358)

So even the idea of a thing we encounter in experience – like a smelly brown goat in the garden – is innate. (The idea has been lying within us, since birth, waiting for the right "prompt" to bring it forward into our consciousness.) The only part of experience that is *not* innate, Descartes writes, is our judgement of the particular circumstances which call up an idea in our minds. So my judgement that I am experiencing the idea of this goat *because* there really is a goat in the garden is a judgement that goes beyond anything that can be found in our storehouse of innate ideas.

One further note on the ideas the intellect can discover. Purely conceptual truths that obtain among ideas – truths such as "Two things equal to a third thing are equal to each other" and "$2 + 3 = 5$" and "A half is less than the whole" – are true at all times, or are true independently of time. Descartes calls them *eternal truths*. Later philosophers have also called them *a priori* truths, or analytic truths. They are truths that nothing in experience can possibly contradict. One would think they are absolutely necessary truths that cannot possibly be false. But, surprisingly, Descartes does not believe that eternal truths are independent of the will of God. He claims – quite carefully – that we cannot say that God does not have the power to create a different universe with a different set of eternal truths. Note the negative way of putting the point: we *cannot* say God *cannot* do it. It is, according to our minds, impossible to conceive of any eternal truth being false; but for all we know, this may be only because God created the universe in a certain way, and our intellects in a certain way, so that what is possible matches up with what we find conceivable. We cannot say what God could not have done. We know only what we can conceive or fail to conceive, given the way God has fashioned our intellects.

KEY POINTS

- Descartes finds he can imagine being wrong about nearly everything except for the fact that his mind exists: "I think (*cogito*), therefore I am."
- Descartes argues that only God could be the cause of his idea of God. And the existence of God in turn guarantees that everything he clearly and distinctly perceives by his mind must be true.
- Descartes thinks we have innate ideas, most notably the idea of God. In one later text, he claims that all ideas are innate, and they are brought to consciousness by the appropriate external conditions.

Dualism

After all this discussion of the intellect and innate ideas, one might wonder whether Descartes has any use at all for the physical world. He does, of course. But before getting to that, we need to understand the relation between the intellect, or mind, and the human body. Descartes distinguishes the two, and thinks of them as independent entities.

In the second meditation, when Descartes discovers the cogito, he affirms his existence as a thinking thing, or a mind. It is not until the last meditation that Descartes is able to prove the existence of his body.

It becomes clear to him that mind and body must be very different things; mind and body must be *distinct substances*, although evidently they work very closely with one another. Descartes generalizes this distinction between mind and body to the rest of the universe: he holds that every thing is either a physical thing (a body) or a mental thing (a mind). This view – that there are two basic kinds of things in reality – is *dualism*.

Here we will need to review some metaphysical terminology. The things in the world, according to Descartes, are *substances*. Intuitively, a substance is a thing that can exist on its own. A ball of wax, for instance, can exist on its own; but its colour, or its firmness or its shape cannot exist by themselves. Descartes would call these dependent qualities of the wax *modes*. The modes of a body change frequently, as bodies shrink, grow and change. But every substance also has one special quality that does not change, an essential quality that the substance cannot lose without going clean out of existence. This special quality is the substance's *principal attribute*. The principal attribute of the ball of wax is its *extendedness*, its quality of having some kind of size. If we were to take away from the wax its quality of having some kind of size – so that it had absolutely no size at all – then we would have turned that piece of wax into nothing.

Extendedness (or, more simply, *extension*) is the "principal attribute" of bodies, according to Descartes. There is one other principal attribute: *thought*, which is the principal attribute of minds. If we take away from a mind its quality of having some kind of thought – so that it had no thought at all – then we would have turned that mind into nothing. The modes of a mind are the particular thoughts, feelings or sensations of the mind, which change frequently. There are two principal attributes, no more and no less; this is another way of characterizing Descartes's dualism.

Substance	Principal attribute	Modes
Some particular body	Extension (having some size)	Particular sizes, shapes, motions
Some particular mind	Thought (being capable of thought)	Particular thoughts, feelings, sensations

We have described particular bodies and minds as substances, since they seem to be things that exist on their own. But more accurately, Descartes thinks of them as "second-class" substances. Strictly speaking, the only thing that can really exist on its own is God. Particular bodies and minds cannot exist without God: God sustains them in existence at each and every moment, and without that sustenance they would vanish immediately. Still, bodies and minds are more self-sufficient than modes are; bodies and minds rely on God for their existence, whereas modes rely both on God and on the bodies or minds to which they belong.

God, according to Descartes, is a mind. God could not be a body and remain infinite and perfect, because bodies are by their nature divisible and hence destructible. God is indestructible; hence God is not extended.

Bodies

There are no empty spaces in the physical world, according to Descartes. This is because space, or extension, is an attribute of bodies, and an attribute cannot exist on its own without belonging to some substance. Space is just not the kind of thing that can exist by itself. It is like *size*: things have size, but *size* cannot exist apart from the thing that has it. So an empty space would be a nothing, with a property – and that, Descartes thinks, is nonsense.

Of course, it often *seems* as if spaces are empty, as when we clear a room or empty a pitcher. But in these cases Descartes says there is always some kind of matter remaining which separates the walls of the room or sides of the pitcher. If there were no matter remaining, then there would be nothing between the walls or sides, and with nothing between them, they necessarily would be in contact with one another. We should be careful here not to think of matter rushing in to fill a gap; this is simply an issue of what space is. Space, again, is an attribute of bodies, and so there cannot be a "disembodied" gap of any size or dimension. Descartes certainly acknowledges, though, that sometimes matter can be so light and thin as to be imperceptible by our senses, and in these cases we might well (mistakenly) judge a space to be completely devoid of matter.

But this raises a question: what makes matter either *heavy* and *thick* or *light* and *thin*? This turns out to be a deep and difficult question in

Descartes's physics. We must remember that Descartes cannot appeal to our understanding of "density", since (with no empty spaces) all matter is equally dense. Descartes can only turn to the *constitution* of bodies: what parts they are made of, and how those parts are configured. Some bodies have parts that are like stacked boxes, and this makes them hard. Other bodies have parts that are like slippery eels, which makes them behave as liquids. And still other bodies have parts that are like the smoothest grains of fine sand, able to pass through the smallest holes – and these bodies behave like gases. The world as a whole may be thought of as a vast expanse of these fine grains of sand, with occasional lumps in it, which are various bodies and liquids. The bodies move and occasionally collide, obeying Descartes's laws of motion and collision, and out of all this matter in motion come all the phenomena of our world. Shape, size and motion – these are the ultimate properties of the extended world.

However, we can still press Descartes on the question of how to distinguish the shapes of the parts of matter. If all matter is ultimately the same kind of stuff, then what makes any part of matter box-like or spherical or eel-like? What makes a body have particular contours? Descartes defines a body as that which moves as a whole through a region. So imagine a crowd of people, and a family of four as they stay close to one another and press through the crowd from one end to the other. The family could be distinguished from the rest of the crowd, and it has a certain family-type shape as it moves through the crowd. But this would mean that as soon as a body stops moving, it becomes indistinguishable from its environment – just as when the family stops, it becomes part of the surrounding crowd. Furthermore, we could well ask what it is that compels the parts of a body to stay together as the body moves. Is it the shape of the body's parts, and the way those parts are hooked together? If so, then this brings us back to our initial question, about what makes those parts have certain shapes. We can call this *the problem of individuating bodies*. Descartes never solved it.

This problem is related to the question of just how many extended substances there really are, according to Descartes. He almost always writes as if each body is a substance. But bodies are distinguished from one another only by motion, which is a mode, and a "modal distinction" is typically not strong enough to mark a difference between substances. (Consider that one body, such as the piece of wax, gains and loses modes over time, and yet we do not infer that it is a different substance.) In one place, in the synopsis of the *Meditations*, Descartes suggests that the whole extended world is a single substance, and bodies are modes of that substance. This view will be important again later when we examine Spinoza's metaphysics.

Motion

Descartes provides laws of motion that describe how bodies move and the ways in which they communicate motion to one another. The chief laws are a principle of inertia and a principle of the conservation of motion. Descartes tries to demonstrate these laws from pure concepts of the intellect: they are thus eternal truths just like the truths of mathematics. But there is a philosophical problem with motion in Descartes's philosophy, beyond the problem of individuating bodies. Motion is a mode of bodies. As bodies collide, they are supposed to communicate motion to one another. But – as it was widely recognized – modes cannot be transferred from one body to another. A mode cannot be separated from its host any more than a particular size or colour could jump off one body, travel through space, and land on another body. So it would seem that motion, as a mode, cannot be transferred from one body to another. We can call this *the problem of body–body causation*, as it concerns the fundamental way in which bodies can cause changes in other bodies.

Descartes tried to solve the problem of body–body causation by turning to his belief that all substances rely on God at each and every moment for their continued existence. If this is so, then as God re-creates the world from moment to moment, he can re-create it in such a way as to make it appear as if motion is being genuinely communicated among colliding bodies. Specifically, when A and B collide and A gives B a certain quantity of motion, what really happens is that God re-creates the world at that moment in such a way that A loses some of its motion and B gains that same amount of motion. So modes are not really transferred from one body to another, and bodies really do not exert causal influence upon one another; the only changes brought about in bodies are brought about by God, on the occasions of certain collisions. Descartes is thus said to be an *occasionalist* with regard to body–body causation, and we shall return to occasionalism later in this chapter.

Still, let us not lose the forest for all the trees. Despite the problems of individuation and body–body causation, and other specific problems with Descartes's particular laws of motion, Descartes's physics is aimed in the right direction. His basic insight is that in the physical world we find only matter in motion. Bodies collide with one another and with us, and those changes in motion are perceived by us as lights, colours, sounds, temperatures, tastes, smells and pressures. But the world itself, as matter in motion, can be described with perfect accuracy by mathematics; and the colours, temperatures and so on of the world are merely in the perceiver, and come about somehow as effects of the fundamental, mathematical phenomena. This is the slogan of the scientific revolution of the seventeenth century.

We should keep in mind that in the generation after Descartes, Isaac Newton will develop a physics based upon similar principles of inertia and the conservation of momentum. If Newton was being genuine when he claimed that he had been able to see what he saw only by standing on the shoulders of giants, then Descartes was one of the giants.

Hylomorphism

In a way, Descartes's chief motivation for constructing his mechanistic physics was to put to rest the medieval, scholastic metaphysics of *hylomorphism*, or "form and matter metaphysics". The scholastics maintained that each substance is a unity of form and matter. The matter is the underlying stuff composing a substance, while the form is what makes the substance the particular kind of thing it is (mineral, vegetable, animal, tiger, man and so on) and also determines the sort of behaviour towards which it is normally inclined. A chunk of earth, for example, because of its form, strives to seek the centre of the universe. The form of a thing can also be identified as its soul, or some organizing principle that gives the substance its nature, direction and purpose. To put the matter most uncharitably – as Descartes often did – the metaphysics of hylomorphism attributes "little souls" to everything, and bases the physics of the world upon the desires and drives of the things in it. Descartes sought to replace this view with his less soulful and more mechanical physics of motion and collision.

To see the difference between the two, imagine two ways of accounting for the heat one feels when sitting near a fire. The scholastics would claim that the fire is composed of some matter and a form, and that the fire is in some way capable of packaging the forms of its colour and heat and smell and sending them to one's body, which receives them, opens the packages, and takes on (in some fashion) those forms of colour and heat and smell. In this way one comes to see the fire, feel its heat, and smell its smell. Descartes's account, on the other hand, is quite different. He would claim that the fire is an excited region of matter, which communicates motion to surrounding particles, and as those motions are communicated to one's skin, pupils and nostrils, one eventually ends up with the perceptions of heat, light and smell.

From our perspective, Descartes's style of explanation has some clear advantages. First, motion can be described and governed by mathematical laws, whereas "forms of heat" and so on cannot. Second, the scholastics will have some difficulty explaining why some observers will have quite different perceptions of the fire. Imagine some other people coming in from a blizzard to enjoy the fire we have built; why should they experience a greater warmth than we do when, according to the scholastic theory, everyone should be receiving the same packages? Descartes can explain these different perceptions by pointing out the different states of motion in the perceivers' bodies: the blizzard people's bodies had been slowed more by the cold, and so they experience a greater excitation of motion within themselves. Finally – and in the end, most importantly – Descartes's style is simpler and provides for a theoretical unity: rather than dozens, hundreds or even thousands of little forms marching about (one per observable quality), we have just motion.

KEY POINTS

- Descartes believes there are ultimately two kinds of things in the world: extended things (bodies), and thinking things (minds). This view is called dualism.
- Size is a property of bodies, so there cannot be a body-less (that is, empty) region of some spatial size.
- Motion cannot be transferred between bodies. But God re-creates bodies from instant to instant in such a way as to make it look as if it is. This view is called occasionalism.
- By basing his physics on size and motion alone, Descartes provides a mathematics-friendly alternative to Aristotelian physics.

Minds

The other substances in the universe (besides bodies) are *minds*. Minds are mirror-opposites of bodies. Minds can think, while bodies cannot. Bodies are extended, while minds are not. And minds are indivisible, while bodies can be divided without limit. In the second meditation, Descartes discovers the mind when he discovers that he is a thinking thing – "a thing that doubts, understands, affirms, denies, is willing, is unwilling, and also imagines and has sensory perceptions". Minds conceive of the world: they represent it to themselves, and they approve or disapprove of what they find. Mere bodies can do none of these things. They have no inwardness, no mentality.

Just as we asked how Descartes individuates bodies, we might wonder how minds are supposed to be individuated. We know all minds have the same attribute, namely thought. Beyond that, their differences are merely modal: one person's individual beliefs and perceptions are different from another's. But of course the same is also true of a single person at different times, so it is hard to see that having different perceptions, ideas or beliefs is enough to make two minds genuinely distinct. Descartes might return to his definition of "substance" and claim that two minds are distinct substances in virtue of the fact that one could be annihilated without destroying the other. But that still does not explain what *makes* them different; it is only another way of announcing the fact *that* they are different from one another. And while Descartes was perhaps willing to say that ultimately there is just one extended substance, he surely did not want to say the same thing about minds. For when it comes to allocating praise and blame and post-earthly destinations, it is important to keep the lines separating individual minds bold and clear.

So we shall suppose along with Descartes that the modal differences are enough for us to individuate minds. Still, what exactly is it that minds do? Overall, they have two spheres of activity: they *think* and they *will*. To think is to frame, explore and consider ideas. The ideas, as we said above, are all innate to the mind, and the mind is able to recall these ideas (under the right conditions), study them, deduce consequences from them, relate them to one another, organize them, and build theories from them. These are the activities of the intellect. At the same time, the mind is capable of affirming or denying these ideas: I can believe an idea, and think of it as true, or deny it and label it as false. These are the actions of the will.

The will

Descartes believes our intellect is limited: at any time, we understand only so many things, and we are often unsure. But he thinks the will is unbounded, in the sense that we are capable of affirming or denying any idea. In this one respect, he thinks, we are like God, who also has an unbounded will. But this is at the same time why we are capable of making mistakes. We are capable of affirming ideas even when our intellects have not been able to obtain any genuine understanding. So we say "Yes" to ideas that are not clear and distinct, and that is how we make mistakes. Note that, after the third meditation, where Descartes undertakes to prove that whatever we clearly and distinctly perceive is true (for God is no deceiver), we cannot really make mistakes by saying "No" to ideas that are clear and distinct, since we no longer have a way to cast doubt upon them.

Descartes offers this account of human error in the fourth meditation, where his chief concern is to reconcile the fact that God made us, and guarantees that what we clearly and distinctly perceive is true, with the fact that we do make mistakes. His reconciliation is that perhaps a creature, in virtue of being a creature, can have only a finite intellect, and that a will cannot be free if it is anything other than unbounded. If a will were restricted in such a way that we could affirm only clear and distinct ideas, then the will would not be playing any genuine role at all; the intellect would be the faculty deciding what we do or do not believe. So, Descartes concludes, our imperfection is in fact consistent with our being created by a perfect being.

But we should note that Descartes treats *freedom* in two different ways. Sometimes "freedom" means the capacity to either affirm or deny, without being restricted in any way to do one or the other. This is a freedom of *indifference*. He calls this a low grade of freedom. A higher grade of freedom is our capacity to affirm ideas that are clear and distinct, or withhold judgement from ideas that are not clear and distinct. When we judge in this way, our judgement is being governed by our reason. Such judgements are considered free because we are not being hoodwinked, duped or coerced by any agent alien to ourselves. We are in these cases free to judge as we see fit. This is a freedom of *spontaneity*, in the sense that our judgements are arising out of ourselves (spontaneously) rather than out of external forces or circumstances. Descartes thinks we have both kinds of freedom, though he prizes spontaneity over indifference. We shall examine these things in greater detail in Chapter 2.

Mind and body

But – to go back to a previous claim – what evidence is there that the human mind and the human body are really distinct things? Descartes offers two arguments.

First, he provides an argument from conceivability. This argument rests on the claim that each can be conceived clearly and distinctly without the other. We can easily imagine a body that does nothing but sits there, extended and unthinking. And we can imagine (or, at least, Descartes thinks we can imagine) an entity that thinks, conceives and imagines without having any size or shape or location; such an entity would be a pure spirit with no physical presence or attachments. If we can conceive these things clearly and distinctly, then they are possible. In other words, it would be possible for God to create a human body without a mind or a mind without a human body. And if one thing *can* exist without another, then the two are genuinely distinct. This argument presumes that there is some kind of link between what we can distinguish in thought and what the world can distinguish in reality. But what guarantees this link? Descartes's answer was given in the third meditation: we know we can trust what we clearly and distinctly perceive, because the perfection and goodness of God would not allow us to be deceived in this regard.

Descartes's second argument focuses on an important difference between bodies and minds. Bodies are divisible. But minds are indivisible, in the sense that we cannot conceive of having only half a thought, or only half of a consciousness, or only half of a perspective upon the world. Now if there is a quality which one thing has and another thing lacks, then this should show that they are not the same thing. And if they are not the same, they are at least in principle separable, and thus genuinely distinct. This argument is perfectly straightforward – though there are some tragic brain-injury cases in psychology that might make us suspect that minds are divisible after all.

We may wish to note that Descartes thought only humans have both minds and bodies. The other animals such as donkeys and giraffes have bodies, but they do not have minds. Descartes regarded non-human animals as something like complicated organic wind-up toys, which were engineered to behave in complex ways, but which did not experience anything or have any degree of consciousness. He has been faulted by later thinkers for encouraging a disregard for the suffering of non-human animals. Indeed, he believed they did not truly suffer at all, no matter what we put them through.

Mind and body interaction

Suppose, then, that the mind and the body are distinct substances. Bodies are extended, material and subject to the laws of nature; minds are not. Minds can frame ideas, entertain suspicions, doubt, deny, affirm, feel, sense and imagine; bodies cannot. They are as distinct as two things can possibly be. Yet it also seems to be true that minds and bodies interact. A mind decides to move, and the body moves. Particles stimulate the retina, and the mind sees a colour. How can there be causal interaction between such completely different kinds of substances?

If we recall Descartes's apparent occasionalism with respect to body–body causation, we might expect that he would present a similar account of mind–body causation. Remember that, according to Descartes, when motion appears to be transferred from one body to another, what really happens is that God takes some motion away from the first body and adds motion to the second body. God, as the great causality broker, surely has the power to cause a similar coordination between what happens in the mind and what happens in the body. Surprisingly, though, the textual evidence suggests that Descartes was not an occasionalist with respect to mind–body causation. Instead, he believes that the mind and the body are in "genuine" causal contact with one another. Perhaps he was worried that, by making God's power a crucial element in mind–body causation, he would be making God morally responsible for the evil decisions humans sometimes make.

In the middle and late 1640s, Princess Elisabeth of Bohemia corresponded with Descartes about mind–body causation. She wondered how it could be possible, according to his metaphysics. Descartes explained that in the middle of the brain there is a thing called the pineal gland, which (he thought) is where all the nerves come together. The pineal gland is surrounded by some very light fluids, called animal spirits. The mind, said Descartes, is able to stir these spirits into motion, thus causing the pineal gland to shift position like a joystick and bring the rest of the body into a particular motion. And, in reverse, if the body's motion causes the pineal gland to move, the animal spirits are stirred, and that motion is communicated to the mind and interpreted as some kind of perception. Still, urged Elisabeth, the mind is immaterial; how can it cause motion in any kind of fluid, no matter how light?

Ultimately Descartes has to answer: "in a way we do not fully understand". But he does not offer this answer immediately. First he takes

Elisabeth for a strange and interesting conceptual ride. He observes that the scholastics had a notion of "heaviness" that in fact was a mix of physical and mental components: bodies are heavy, said the scholastics, because their primary component, earth, strives to seek the centre of the universe. In this idea of "heaviness" there are equal material and mentalistic contributions, inasmuch as within the matter of the earth itself is the desire to reach its natural resting place. Now Descartes does not for even a minute endorse this scholastic understanding of "heaviness", but he recognizes that God must have implanted this strange crossbred idea into our heads for some good reason. But he thinks it was not to understand the downward motion of bodies. Instead, he suggests, this is the notion that should be applied to the case of mind–body interaction. God supplies us with this strange combined mental/physical notion so that we can conceive how the human mind and the body are integrated into a substantial union. The scholastics merely stuck the idea into the wrong spot in their theory.

Descartes is surely way out on a limb with this speculation, but it is brilliant: he skewers the scholastics and gets a hook into his own solution with a single harpoon. But when Elisabeth presses for further details, Descartes has to plead humble and reverent ignorance.

Without an answer to this question, every interaction between mind and body is a sheer miracle. The mind getting the brain to move is no less miraculous than its getting a spoon to bend. And the brain sending information to the conscious mind is as miraculous (and unthinkable) as a locomotive sharing its feelings with us. Descartes cracked the universe in two, and never managed to build a bridge.

Key points

- Descartes divides the universe into a world of mechanistic bodies and a world of immaterial minds.
- God is the creator of this world, governing all physical interactions and guaranteeing that the structure of the human mind mirrors the fundamental structure of the world.
- The mind and the body are completely unlike one another, but they somehow are able to interact with one another; Descartes was never able to explain how this is possible.

two

Descartes's morals and *The Passions of the Soul*

The place of morals in Descartes's philosophy

Descartes is remembered mostly for his contributions in epistemology, metaphysics and physics. Yet by his own account, these philosophical discoveries have value only to the extent that they allow us to improve our lives and gain moral excellence. "Thus the whole of philosophy is like a tree," he wrote in his *Principles of Philosophy*. "The roots are metaphysics, the trunk is physics, and the branches emerging from the trunk are all the other sciences, which may be reduced to three principal ones, namely medicine, mechanics, and morals" (AT IXB, 14). And he continued: "By 'morals' I understand the highest and most perfect moral system, which presupposes a complete knowledge of the other sciences and is the ultimate level of wisdom." And so, although he wrote comparatively little about morals (and not much on medicine and mechanics either), he took morality to be one of the great and final ends of his philosophy. After all, he viewed it as the ultimate level of wisdom.

The first time Descartes laid down some moral rules was in his *Discourse on Method*, published in 1637 when he was 41 years old. We should keep in mind that in this work, as in the *Meditations*, Descartes is pretending to chronicle his adventures as a clear-minded pilgrim seeking the truth. His goal is to discover what he is certain of – what is ultimately real, whether there is a god, who and what he really is, and so on. But in the *Discourse*, before he travels very far down this road, he pauses to set some guidelines for his life while he is in the process of trying to doubt all of his previous beliefs. His worry is that he might do himself some real harm if he ends up trying to make important decisions in his life while in the midst of his deep and pervasive doubt. So he sets up a "provisional moral code" – a code he can live by while he undertakes his investigation, like a small shelter one can take refuge in while rebuilding a house. He sets forward three maxims:

> 1. To obey the laws and customs of my country, holding constantly to the religion in which by God's grace I had been instructed from my childhood, and governing myself in all other matters according to the most moderate and least extreme opinions. (AT VI, 23)

> 2. To be as firm and decisive in my actions as I could, and to follow even the most doubtful opinions, once I had adopted them, with no less constancy than if I had been quite certain.
> (AT VI, 24)

> 3. To always try to master myself rather than fortune, and change my desires rather than the order of the world.
> (AT VI, 25)

These are maxims he thought he could follow no matter what outward form his life took, whether he became a soldier, lawyer or scientist. But at the same time, he made a firm decision about the direction his life should take:

> Without wishing to say anything about the occupations of others, I thought I could do no better than to continue with the very one I was engaged in, and devote my whole life to cultivating my reason and advancing as far as I could in the knowledge of the truth. (AT VI, 27)

He decided to be a philosopher.

But Descartes was largely silent about ethics for about eight years following this publication. He published the *Meditations* and the *Principles* (with the tree analogy given above), and wrote many letters, but does not indicate anywhere that he has moved beyond this provisional moral code. Then, in 1645, in his correspondence with Princess Elisabeth of Bohemia, he pours out more reflections about morality. And, finally, in his last publication, *The Passions of the Soul* (1649), he delivers his moral psychology.

Why the lapse, and why then the surge of interest? The lapse is due no doubt to the energy he devoted to his metaphysics, physics, epistemology and theology. In the years 1637–45 he was completely consumed by these efforts. But these efforts to redirect Western philosophy landed him in a good deal of controversy. He was attacked by several theologians, and he fought back with equal ferocity. At the same time, over these years he became acquainted with grief: his daughter Francine died in 1640 at the age of five. These events must have forced him into serious reflection about the way he should lead his life: what he should form attachments to, and what he should remain free from. And, as a man in the middle of his natural life, he probably turned towards questions about what in life is significant and what is fleeting. When Princess Elisabeth began to ask him questions raised by the complications in her own life, she found a man who was asking himself many of the same questions.

In the rest of this chapter we shall examine these later reflections on morality. But first we should observe that a certain ethic exercised a global pull over Descartes's philosophy from the very beginning. He decided early on to turn inward, to hide himself in remote areas, and devote his mind to an ideal realm of pure bodies and immaterial souls. Of course, he was no hermit, and he did seek fame for his achievements. But he did not want his notoriety to break through the soft tranquillity padding his life. In that peaceful shelter, he sought to discipline his mind and his passions so that he could control as much of his experience as possible, and, where that failed, control his reactions to what life dealt him. He was, in short, a stoic: he sought to lead a life of reasonable self-control, with an inner safe harbour to protect him in case of any storm.

The provisional moral code

Many readers have found Descartes's first maxim underwhelming. Descartes was a bold and radical thinker, doubting what centuries of philosophers had maintained as certainly true, resolving to – well, resolving more or less to go along with the crowd and stay firmly in the mainstream as much as possible. Can anything be said about this maxim to connect it with the revolutionary character of Descartes's thought, or the extraordinary depth of his metaphysical investigations?

We must keep in mind the occasion that calls Descartes to lay down these provisional principles. He is about to embark on a deep investigation of what is true and what is false, and he needs some rules to keep him out of trouble. He thinks it will be safe if he tries to stay in the mainstream of his own local culture, country and religion. And, indeed, that is a safe bet, in at least two ways. First, it is safe because it will not attract the attention of zealous enforcers of societal and religious rules. (We should bear in mind that Descartes had just withdrawn publication of *The World*, after seeing what had happened to Galileo.) Second, it is safe because, at this stage, he is not equipped to provide anything better than the morals offered by the world around him, and for all he knows the moral code everyone else is following may be the right one. If you are lost in a field and there is one beaten path, you may as well follow it, even if there are dozens of other possible directions you could take and even if you are not sure it leads to where you want to go. In all likelihood, the trail is there for some reason.

To these observations regarding the safety of the first maxim we may add a couple more. First, to the extent that following the morality of one's society affects only one's outward behaviour, staying in the mainstream allows for a greater freedom of mind. In short: if you want uninterrupted thought, you will get more of it by conforming to others' social expectations than by trying to reform the society around you. "Just get along," runs the idea, "and do not cause others to interrupt the peace you need to carry out your meditations." Perhaps this is selfish or dishonest. But until Descartes discovers for himself what he thinks is true, he does not feel equipped to challenge the status quo. His best bet is to lie low until he feels that he has a better understanding of how he should live. The second observation is that a moral theme running through Descartes's life is "to try to master myself rather than the world" (as stated in the third maxim). Very few of us will be able to change the morality or religion of the culture in which we are raised, even if we wanted to. But any of us can accommodate our outward lives to those practices, and then find a private space within our lives to do what we regard as most meaningful. (Or at any rate this is true if we are fortunate enough not to live in any of the world's most oppressive societies; Descartes thought he was this fortunate, and on the whole he was right.)

With these observations, Descartes's first maxim is indeed radical, mostly for what it does not say. It does *not* tell us to regard our own society or religion as especially authoritative, and it does *not* tell us to revere where we happen to be born as the place to find the best morality. Instead, it simply recommends that we give our society its due, so as to give ourselves the maximal freedom in which to philosophize. It tells us that our individual pursuits of philosophy are actually more significant than anything society will ask of us. Thus we should do what little we need to do in order to get by in our society, so that privately we can devote our efforts towards what is really important.

Indeed, the second maxim amplifies this attitude: "To be as firm and decisive in my actions as I could, and to follow even the most doubtful opinions, once I had adopted them, with no less constancy than if I had been quite certain" (AT VI, 24). In effect, Descartes tells us, "When you have to make a decision, make it and stick to it; that will be simpler than having to revisit the decision again and again." Moreover, as Descartes writes, our minds will be less troubled if we resolve firmly to carry through our decisions:

> By following this maxim I could free myself from all the regrets and remorse which usually trouble the consciences of those weak and faltering spirits who allow themselves to set out on some supposedly good course of action which later, in their inconstancy, they judge to be bad. (AT VI, 25)

Note that Descartes's primary concern here is not whether our decisions and actions actually are good or not. In fact, given the situation he is in, he does not feel competent to judge that matter. His primary concern is to set down practical rules for a life as free from friction and from obvious error as possible. He says his situation is like that of a man lost in the woods. He does not know which direction is right, but he knows that if he does not march decisively in a straight line he will remain lost. In this case – a less than optimal one, to be sure – deciding and acting with resolve is far better than continually going back and reconsidering one's own strategy. And, besides, he thinks we shall be happier if we stick with our decisions instead of continually revisiting them and wondering if we decided upon the right thing. As Descartes later writes, "Nothing causes regret and remorse except irresolution" (AT IV, 295).

In all, Descartes's provisional morality is designed for the philosophical lifestyle. If we want to discover for ourselves what is true and valuable, and if we think the way to go about it is through intensely private meditation, then we will want a code that minimizes friction with the outside world and maximizes our freedom for philosophical reflection. There is every possibility that, in all this reflection, we shall eventually discover a more substantial moral code. And this is the sense in which Descartes's moral code is only "provisional": it provides us with a structure for our lives that makes it possible for us to discover an even more suitable structure for our lives – if there is any such structure.

Happiness

Descartes's moral philosophy is grounded in a particular conception of human happiness. Reasonably enough, Descartes came to believe that one's life should be directed towards a wholesome and lasting contentment. Possessing that happiness is what makes a human life a good one. Later in his life, in a work called *The Passions of the Soul*, Descartes undertook a psychological investigation into human emotions with the aim of discovering how we can regulate our lives and thoughts so that we can become happy and remain so. We shall examine this work later in this chapter. But for now, it is important to get a better understanding of what Descartes thinks happiness is.

In 1645, Descartes corresponded with his friend, Princess Elisabeth of Bohemia, about the nature of happiness. They were reading Seneca's *On the Happy Life* together and exchanging letters about it. Descartes thought Seneca (*c.* 2 BCE–65 CE) understood happiness about as well as any pagan philosopher could, and he used this occasion to correct Seneca and offer his own thoughts on happiness as well. Seneca observed that all of us want to be happy, but few of us really understand what makes a life happy. Descartes agreed, and points out that what Seneca means by "the happy life" can be understood in two ways. First, it could mean the *fortunate* or *lucky* life. Second, it could mean the *satisfied* life, or the life that is arranged in such a way that the person living it is content with whatever luck brings. Descartes thinks the satisfied life is far superior to the lucky one, and we will be happiest if we pursue it.

Later, in *The Passions of the Soul*, Descartes explains why he believes this. First, there is the problem that no one can count on being lucky; by definition, it is beyond our control. But more importantly, Descartes thinks that by hoping and wishing for luck in our lives, we will be distracted from the things we can do to make our lives happier and make ourselves satisfied. Imagine someone, for example, who thinks of nothing but the wonderful things she will buy when she wins the lottery. She makes elaborate plans, and every week buys a promising set of lottery tickets. She does little else but chase this dream. The odds are stacked heavily against her winning, of course, and while she is chasing this dream she is neglecting all of the immediate things she could do to make her life happier. She could be saving her money, for example, to buy special items now and then, and she could be hosting modest parties for her friends. But she has traded these simple and certain pleasures for a distant and improbable fantasy, and as a result her life is far less happy.

(Assuming, of course, that in the end she does not win the lottery! What would Descartes say if she did? How would the happiness of a supremely lucky life compare with the happiness in a satisfied life? It seems as if nothing beats a lot of luck. But even so, there may be some kinds of pleasures that come from leading a satisfied life, pleasures that no amount of luck can produce. Later we shall see why Descartes thinks these pleasures may even exceed all the varied pleasures luck can bring.)

If we identify happiness with satisfaction, then Descartes thinks that all people are capable of attaining happiness. He recognizes that some lives have more misfortune in them than others – lives with severe sickness, for example, or other physical maladies, or extreme poverty. But nevertheless he thinks that within each life there is the possibility of attaining full contentment, once the person living the life has made her desires and appetites conform to her own capacities and to what she may reasonably expect from life. As he writes to Elisabeth:

> a small vessel may be just as full as a large one, although it contains less liquid; and similarly if we regard each person's contentment as the full satisfaction of his desires duly regulated by reason, I do not doubt that the poorest people, least blest by nature and fortune, can be entirely content and satisfied just as much as everyone else, although they do not enjoy as many good things. (AT IV, 264–5)

This remark reveals an important ingredient for Cartesian happiness: *reason*. Happiness, according to Descartes, is not simply reached through the satisfaction of all one's desires, but through the satisfaction of all the desires *reason* has approved. This makes sense if we are looking only towards the satisfied life, and not the lucky one. Trying to live a satisfied life means aiming only towards those pleasures we may be reasonably confident of reaching. Each life may have a different set of pleasures to be aimed for: the pleasures available to a princess, for example, will be very different from those available to a hunchbacked bell-ringer. But the princess and the bell-ringer can each attain the pleasures available to them (hosting grand balls, ringing great bells), and so long as their reason does not allow them to expect more than the pleasures they can reach, then Descartes believes that each of them may become "entirely content and satisfied". Pursuing happiness under the guidance of reason means restricting your desires to what you might actually have a chance of obtaining. Anyone can do this, Descartes says, and so anyone can be as happy as anyone else.

At this point, Descartes's optimism may sound quite implausible and even ludicrous. Would this view not lead to the outrageous conclusion that a starving and diseased beggar can be as fully happy as the richest, healthiest emperor? But once we examine some further features of his psychology and his moral theory, we will be able to appreciate the sentiment Descartes is proposing. First, though, we shall need to see what role reason plays in Descartes's theory of happiness.

Reason

Just after providing the vessel analogy in his letter to Elisabeth, Descartes offers three conditions for satisfaction which he says are related to the provisional moral code he offered in the *Discourse*. But these conditions are importantly different from the provisional moral code, and the differences have everything to do with *reason*. The rules are as follows:

1. You should employ your mind as well as you can to discover what you should do or not do in all the circumstances of life.
2. You should resolve firmly and resolutely to carry out whatever reason recommends without being distracted by passions and appetites.
3. You should not concern yourself with anything shown by reason to be utterly unavailable to you.

Perhaps this moral code is the more permanent shelter Descartes sought to establish while living in the temporary abode of his provisional moral code. Recall that the earlier code told us to avoid all unnecessary friction with the outside world, adapting our lives to society's expectations as much as we can, so that we can engage in deep philosophical meditation without being distracted by conflict. This newer code opens the door to a greater range of conflict, since what reason dictates may be quite different from what society dictates. But there is a broad similarity in the two codes: the first asks us to conform to society's expectations, and the second asks us to conform to reason's expectations. It is as if we need to grow up under the shelter of our elders, but once our reason matures we can judge for ourselves.

How does reason help us make good choices? It can help us in three ways. First, as we develop our knowledge of human psychology and medicine, we gain better knowledge of what really is healthy for us and what really harms us. Second, once we know what is good for us, we can then design practices and therapies to incorporate into our lives so that we are less likely to give in to those desires that will put us in harm's way. Finally, reason will help us to form a clearer picture of what we can change and what we will simply have to live with. This last service is captured in the prayer commonly used by people struggling with various addictions: "Lord, give us grace to accept with serenity the things that cannot be changed, courage to change the things which should be changed, and the wisdom to distinguish the one from the other." Living reasonably means limiting our desires to what we can reasonably expect to obtain.

According to Descartes, we shall not be able to live satisfied lives unless we use our reason. In fact, reason is so important that he has to retract what he said earlier with his analogy of the vessels, about all people being able to be happy, regardless of circumstance. If someone loses his reason, then happiness will be impossible for him – "it is less distressing to lose one's life than to lose use of one's reason", Descartes opines (AT IV, 282), since only those of us armed with reason will be able to know the way to obtain satisfaction.

Reason's job is to discover the true goods, not just the things that happen to feel good at the time. But what makes something a "true" good, according to Descartes? The answer has to do with perfection.

Perfection, virtue and generosity

We experience various pleasures and pains. Initially we might try to follow the simple rule of pursuing the pleasures and avoiding the pains. But we soon discover that some pleasures are caused by things that are in fact bad for us and some pains are caused by things that are good for us. The things that really are good for us are *perfections*, according to Descartes.

This term requires some explanation. In order to understand it, we first need to distinguish qualities that exist because of the *presence* of something from qualities that exist because of the *absence* of something. Heat, for example, exists because of the presence of rapidly jiggling motions among molecules. Cold, on the other hand, exists only when those jiggling motions are absent. When there is no jiggling at all, we are at absolute zero. Light, as a second example, indicates the presence of some energy source, and darkness indicates the lack of an energy source. A perfection according to Descartes will turn out to be a *real something*, not the absence or lack of a real something.

Second, we need to understand that, according to Descartes, the reality of all things in the world – in other words, the world's perfection – is due ultimately to the presence of God. God himself has all perfections – all the "somethings" that are genuinely and ultimately real: power, knowledge, wisdom, love, justice and so on. When God creates things, he puts some perfection or reality into them. But all God's creatures are finite, so each one is lacking something. These various lackings are what make the created world so imperfect. Everything that is wrong with the world is due to creatures' lack of God's perfections. The absence of God is the presence of evil.

Now we can explain what perfections are in the case of human beings. As creatures of God, we possess limited quantities of God's perfections. We have some power, some knowledge, some wisdom and so on. These are perfections. Since we are finite, we also have weaknesses, ignorance, foolishness and bad intentions. These are imperfections – our shortcomings – and we have them simply as a result of being finite. To the extent that we can encourage the growth of our perfections, we come to be more godly, which is a good thing.

To grow in our perfections is to grow in *virtue*, according to Descartes. Our chief virtue is to use our reason and our freedom in order to make good choices and grow in our perfections. Making virtuous decisions is the key to all other virtues. Becoming virtuous is our target, says Descartes. And our reward for hitting the target is contentment of mind, as he tells Elisabeth:

> In order to achieve a contentment which is solid, we need to pursue virtue – that is to say, to maintain a firm and constant will to bring about everything we judge to be the best, and to use all the power of our intellect in judging well. (AT IV, 277)

This means that as we go through life our goal should not be just to pile up one joy after another. Rather, we should aim towards being virtuous, since by being virtuous we shall thereby gain the greatest kind of happiness, which is this solid contentment of mind.

Why does this contentment come along with being virtuous? In *The Passions of the Soul*, Descartes explains that the feeling of joy is a certain "excitation" in the soul which occurs when it judges that it possesses some good. Of course sometimes we make mistakes about what is good for us, and so sometimes we feel joy when we really should not. But when we are not considering the prizes and spoils brought by luck, and are considering just the goods that can come to us through our own efforts, we can be relatively sure that we are in the possession of a true good, and not one that can be taken from us by bad luck. So, for example, we can always feel good about having been kind to someone who deserved kindness. We cannot always feel good about our new bicycle – especially after it has been stolen.

The special kind of joy that comes from our own efforts Descartes calls *generosity*. The term "generosity" is supposed to mean something like "magnanimity" or "having an excellent soul". As Descartes writes in *The Passions of the Soul*, a person's generosity consists:

> partly in his understanding that there is nothing which truly belongs to him but this free control of his volitions, and no reason why he ought to be praised or blamed except that he uses it well or badly; and partly in his feeling within himself a firm and constant resolution to use it well, that is, never to lack the volition to undertake and execute all the things he judges to be best – which is to follow virtue perfectly. (AT IV, 446)

To be generous is to know that we have done what should be done – we have judged well, acted wisely and made the best of things. This yields a distinct joy, the joy that comes from knowing that we have lived well through the exercise of our own powers.

This, finally, is why Descartes thinks the highest happiness is available to all who can govern their lives by reason. For if we follow reason, we shall be capable of Cartesian generosity and capable of living virtuously, no matter what our circumstances may be. In this respect, the princess and the bell-ringer can be equally happy, so long as each has lived as well as circumstances permit. Of course, the other pleasures will be unequal – fancy pastries versus thin gruel – but (Descartes would presumably say) these sorts of joys are not significant when compared to the joy of generosity. And, from a certain perspective, he would be right – though we may wish to insist that those other joys do count, at least a little.

We can see also why Descartes thinks the satisfied life may have greater happiness in it than the supremely lucky life. Only the satisfied life can have generosity in it – that feeling of self-assurance, the knowledge that we have made good decisions and we have done everything in our power to live virtuously. Luck cannot bring that kind of satisfaction. And perhaps Descartes would add that no quantity of joys won through luck can equal the joy that comes from generosity.

Reason's dictates

In their correspondence, Elisabeth asks Descartes what reason can teach us regarding the virtuous life. Descartes offers two prescriptions: know the truth, and practise remembering this knowledge and assenting to it whenever the occasion demands. He then goes on to list some of the truths it is useful for us to keep in mind if we are to make virtuous choices:

1. We need to remember that there is a God on whom all things depend, and that we should accept calmly all the things that happen to us as sent by God.
2. We need to know that we have a soul that survives the body. This will help us not to fear death, and it will help us to detach our interests from material things.
3. It is important to know just how vast the universe is. This will keep us humble, as we bear in mind that God may have bigger concerns than our own.
4. We should bear in mind that we are part of several larger wholes: the family, the society, the state and the universe. Each part relies on the others, and so we are as reliant on fellow human beings as they are on us. Sometimes the interests of the whole will outweigh the interests of one of its members, so we should expect not always to get our way.
5. We should know that our complex psychology can often deceive us, and that many pleasures may seem to be greater than they really are. "We should not let ourselves easily be deceived by the false appearance of the goods of this world."
6. Finally – and this last truth should be contrasted with Descartes's provisional moral code – we should carefully examine what society expects of us and use our reason to determine to what extent we should try to meet these expectations. At the same time, we need to recognize that we cannot have certain demonstrations for everything, and sometimes it may be better simply to follow custom than to second-guess our decisions and actions.

What kind of lives shall we lead if we keep these things in mind? Descartes believes we shall come to value health, joy and knowledge. We shall take delight in beautiful objects, and welcome friendship with other human beings since they can help us in many ways and bring great delight to us. We shall be tolerant of life's misfortunes, because we know that things cannot always go our way, and we are confident that God has an overall plan. We shall, above all, prize our capacity for free choice, in ourselves and in others, as it allows us to choose to live virtuously, and we shall be grateful to God for endowing us with that capacity. We shall make the wisest choices we can and stick to them, and we shall not reproach ourselves so long as we are sure that we made the best decision we could in our particular circumstance. We shall not fear death, but take pleasure in life – at least so far as reason allows.

The generous human being – Descartes's moral ideal – closely resembles the wise man praised by Seneca. Such a human being portions off what he can control from what he cannot. So far as he is able, he uses reason to make wise decisions regarding his conduct and his life's direction. At the same time, he realizes that fortune and luck may bring all kinds of surprises into his life. He prepares for them as best he can, and tries merely to endure what he cannot avoid. In times of affliction, he comforts himself in the recognition that he has done the best he can, and that everything else is in the hands of a divine providence.

We may note, though, that Descartes's ethics at least so far is almost completely self-centred. The generous human being may well help others or lend service to her community, but only under two conditions: (1) when the generous person is in a community that expects her to do this (since there is some incentive to have good relations with one's community), or (2) when it is to the generous person's own benefit to do so. The generous person might go out and pick up litter, for instance, but only for the reason that she herself prefers not to see litter on the ground, and not necessarily because she feels the duty to do so, or because she is concerned for others' well-being. The generous person might take a kind of intellectual joy in seeing others exercise virtue, but not out of a kind of empathy for them. Instead, the generous person is happy simply to see a life that is well lived, as we take joy in seeing a tennis match well played. The generous person is quite self-centred, though in all fairness it must be added that her concern for herself leads her to leading an exemplary life. She has no reason to take an interest in others for their own sake.

KEY POINTS

- According to Descartes, the good life for human beings is the one with the greatest happiness in it.
- We become happy by getting what is truly good for us. Reason allows us to discern the true goods and discover ways to obtain them. Reason also recommends that we understand our limitations, try not to expect too much, and face any disappointments with equanimity.
- The highest human good is virtue, which we exercise by making good judgements and trying to bring about what is best, so far as this is possible.
- Being virtuous brings us the greatest joy, which Descartes calls "generosity", or having an excellent soul.

Passions of the soul

At Elisabeth's request, Descartes wrote a short work explaining how various human emotions come about and how we can try to cope with them in order to lead virtuous lives. That work was *The Passions of the Soul*, and it was the last work Descartes published.

In coming to understand this work, we first need to understand what Descartes means by "passion". A passion is anything that happens to a person. We are "passive" with respect to them. We can be affected by things outside our bodies, as when acorns fall on our heads and we feel *pain*. Or we can be affected by things internal to ourselves, as when we reflect on something we should not have done and feel *regret*. Pain and regret are passions – the feelings happen to us whether we want them or not – and Descartes's main objective in *The Passions of the Soul* is to teach us what is going on when we experience them, and how to manage our reactions to them.

The human body, according to Descartes, is a complex organic machine. In principle, we could develop a nearly complete mechanical account of what keeps the heart beating, the blood circulating, the muscles moving, and the various chemicals being produced. With this account we could explain all autonomic functions (digestion, secretion, pulse and so on) and all reflex actions. But we could not account for all human behaviour, Descartes would say, because some effects in the body are brought about not by mechanical causes but by the soul. When an acorn drops on my head, a signal is sent to my brain, and specifically to the pineal gland in the middle of my brain, which is moved in a certain direction. That motion is somehow coordinated with a conscious perception in my soul of sudden pain. *If there is no intervention by the soul*, the motion of the pineal gland will lead quite automatically to further events in my body: nerve signals will instruct my face to wince, my mouth to say "ouch", my hand to come up and rub my head, and so on. But suppose I am in a situation in which I do not wish to call attention to myself (I am sneaking up on someone). In that case, my soul can deliberately override what would otherwise follow automatically from the acorn incident, and I can maintain a stony silence (perhaps permitting myself a slight wince). I cannot will myself not to feel the pain, but I can moderate my behaviour in response to it.

The same kind of account can be given of many human experiences. For the most part, we cannot help but have these experiences (though in some cases we can distract ourselves from minor pains so as not to endure them). But very often we can control our behaviour in response to them.

> The most the will can do while this excitation [from a passion] is in full strength is not to consent to its effects and to restrain many of the movements to which it disposes the body. For example, if anger makes the hand rise in order to strike, the will can ordinarily restrain it; if fear incites the legs to flee, the will can stop them. (AT IV, 295)

So we may distinguish what would ordinarily or naturally happen as the result of a passion from what happens as a result of the interference of the soul. Strictly speaking, each time the soul interferes with the body's natural inclinations, something of a miracle occurs: the pineal gland normally would move *this* way, but instead some supernatural entity (the immaterial soul) causes the gland *not* to move that way. This is why there cannot be a complete mechanical account of human behaviour. When the soul goes to work, miracles happen.

Salvation – or at any rate *virtue* – depends on these miracles. For the soul is the thing making wise decisions in accordance with reason, and freeing our bodies from being slaves to the passions. These decisions show up in the body as naturally inexplicable motions of the pineal gland. Here, of course, the objections raised in Chapter 1 take hold: just how can the immaterial soul move a physical thing like the pineal gland? How can the motion of the gland communicate a particular passion to the soul? In the end, Descartes found no answer to these questions. The best he can do is insist that God has implanted in us a special notion of mind–body unity which the scholastics misapplied throughout their metaphysics of hylomorphism.

Genealogy of the passions

In *The Passions of the Soul*, Descartes lists about forty different passions (such as wonder, scorn, pride, humility, hope, desire, despair and so on). After reviewing them, he hypothesizes that there are only six basic passions, and all the rest are variants of them. The six primitive passions are wonder, love, hatred, desire, joy and sadness. In other words, the six primitive passions are like the alphabet of experience: by combining them in various ways we obtain the full and rich prose of our emotional lives.

Pain, for example, is a kind of very sudden sadness which typically indicates to us that the body has been damaged in some way. Anger is a kind of sadness caused by the perception of some evil someone has done to us. Hope is the recognition of some likelihood that something we desire will come to us. Laughter is a moderate kind of joy, mixed sometimes with wonder and other times with hatred, depending on the kind of laughter it is. And so on, Descartes thinks, with all human passions. Each one of them can be traced to some combination of the primitive passions. Most of *The Passions of the Soul* is bound up with tracing through this genealogy of the passions, partly just to explain the passions as natural phenomena, and partly to educate us about the conditions that are likely to cause various passions within us. When we learn, for example, that mockery is caused by a joy arising from our observation that some evil befalls someone who deserves it, we might then come to recognize that feeling in ourselves from time to time, and we might subsequently decide that we should not always follow our inclination to mock other people if we feel that we should not express joy at another's misfortune.

Descartes also relates our various passions to physiological states. When we feel a surprising wonder coupled with joy, for instance, the heart opens up and more blood pours out into the arteries and the lungs swell; the swelling then forces some sudden changes in muscles in the chest, throat and face, and at the same time forces air suddenly through the windpipe; as a consequence of all this, we *laugh*. This physiological reaction can be stopped only through some singularly strong act of will, or by training ourselves over time to control these reactions.

Descartes recognizes that not all of us react in the same way to similar passions. Not all brains are disposed in the same manner, he says, and experiences may provide us with different lessons about what is good and what is evil, and what is desirable and what is not. The account he provides is true for most of us, he thinks, although he is willing to grant that there can be variations.

General remedy for the passions

A summary of the advice Descartes gives in *The Passions of the Soul* can be found near the end of the work:

> When one feels the blood stirred up like that, one should take warning, and recall that everything presented to the imagination tends to deceive the soul, and to make the reasons for favoring the object of its Passion appear to it much stronger than they are, and those for opposing it much weaker. And when the Passion favors only things whose execution admits of some delay, one must abstain from making any immediate judgment about them, and distract oneself by other thoughts

> until time and rest have completely calmed the excitation of the blood. Finally, when it incites one to actions requiring one to reach some resolution at once, the will must be inclined above all to take into consideration and to follow the reasons opposed to those the Passion represents, even though they appear less strong. (AT XI, 487)

So, in short: never act while in the grip of a passion, if you can afford some delay to cool down and think it over. And in cases where you cannot delay, be sure to test your feelings against other feelings that recommend a different action. If you are seized by fear and are moved to run, try to drum up passions of honour and valour that would encourage you to stand firm. Weigh the contradictory passions, and make the best decision you can under the circumstances.

We can see from this advice that Descartes thinks passions are never exactly overpowered by reason alone. The best we can do is get ourselves to wait until a passion subsides, so that reason can then determine our actions. Or if we cannot wait, we fight fire with fire: that is, we line up an equal and opposite passion to try to mitigate the influence of the first passion, and hope that we will be steered towards a more rational course of action. So, for example, if we feel nervous about speaking in public, we might try to overcome the fear we feel by trying to imagine the members of our audience as naked – and that imaginative device somehow makes us feel a kind of superiority over them, lessening the fear we otherwise would feel. That is one way of employing one passion to tame another.

According to Descartes, this is simply the situation we are stuck with as embodied creatures. Each day we must enter into negotiation with all of the various pulls and pushes the material world and our bodies present to us. Through the careful employment of our reason, and the careful deployment of our own inclinations towards passions, we may steer a steady course.

KEY POINTS

- There are six basic passions: wonder, love, hatred, desire, joy and sadness. All the other passions are built from these basic ones.
- We cannot escape feeling the passions, but (sometimes with great training) we can control our behaviours in response to them.
- We should never act in haste, but only after we have consulted our reason.

Religion

We may recall that Descartes thought Seneca presented a morality about as good as any "pagan" could. This might lead us to ask what role religion plays in Descartes's own philosophy. How is Descartes's religious knowledge supposed to put him in any better place than Seneca?

In fact this question lies at the heart of the intellectual controversies Descartes faced in his life. His critics could not see that Descartes's philosophy relied heavily upon the revealed truths of Christianity. Descartes argues for God's existence, and makes God causally responsible for our existence and the world's existence at all crucial points, but it may be objected that there is nothing particularly *religious* about Descartes's God. One could be a thorough Cartesian, it seems, and find no need ever to pray or go to church or seek forgiveness for one's sins. Descartes's God is more the God of the philosophers than the God of the Bible.

One defence that Descartes often offered was that he was only trying to lay out what our reason can tell us about God. He nowhere denies any of the beliefs promoted by the Church. He sees those beliefs as *beyond reason* – they are not necessarily irrational, but reason does not have the power to demonstrate them, and they must be accepted by faith. Christianity can be "added on" to Cartesian philosophy without any conflict, just as Descartes's great medieval predecessor, Thomas Aquinas, synthesized Christianity with Aristotle's philosophy. Descartes is simply trying to modernize the "natural" end of things, leaving the rest of revealed doctrine intact.

But at the same time it is clear that Descartes's Christianity meant a great deal to him and to his philosophy. His correspondence reveals that he took his religion very seriously, and not just out of a practical fear of condemnation and punishment. He stakes out controversial positions on whether God has power over the so-called eternal truths and the metaphysics of the Eucharist. In his published works and in his letters, he rarely misses an opportunity to thank God for any perfections we have and to credit God with the many wonderful things we find in the world. It is sensible to conclude that Descartes's vision of reality reserved a very important place for God as the creator and sustainer of reality, and the source upon whom all goodness depends. At the same time, he may have been somewhat sceptical or even cynical about all the political manoeuvrings of the churches of his day, as this was a time when Catholic and Protestant authorities wielded considerable political and economic power; and where there is power, there is often corruption and abuse of that power. In keeping with his general moral outlook, Descartes tried to distance himself from the intrigue and focus his attention on a purer land of contemplation, one that would not be upset by the ravages of fortune.

Moreover, religion does play a significant role in Descartes's moral advice. Believing that there is a God, and that the universe is made according to a divine plan, helps us calmly to accept those things that seem to go against our best interest. We then would have reason to believe that all things in life, even those that upset us terribly, are part of God's plan. And believing that we have an immortal soul helps us face death, and to behave bravely in dangerous circumstances. Furthermore, it may be that the Christian gospel, particularly the injunction to love one's neighbour as oneself, provides Descartes's ethics with a genuine concern for others, a concern it would otherwise lack. This would be an instance where a revealed truth gives an individual something more than what reason alone provides. Descartes, however, says nothing about this particular aspect of Christian doctrine. In the end – apart from the friendliness of many of his letters – we do not have much evidence that he ever really was much concerned with others.

Key points

- Descartes's moral outlook is broadly Stoic in character: controlling one's life under the guidance of reason is the most secure route to happiness.
- We obtain happiness by aiming at virtue, which is the art of judging wisely and bringing about the best. When we do this, we experience the deep joy Descartes calls "generosity".
- Descartes's morality is fundamentally self-centred, since we are interested in being virtuous only for our own happiness.
- Religion helps us to lead the moral life in so far as it gives us hope (for an afterlife) and keeps mundane matters in a cosmic perspective.

three

Spinoza's one substance

Biography

Baruch de Spinoza was born into a Jewish family in Amsterdam in 1632. His parents had moved from Portugal to Amsterdam in order to escape the Catholic Church's persecution of Jews. In Amsterdam the family joined a large Jewish community which was tolerated – within some sharp limits – by the surrounding Christian populace. Spinoza's mother died when he was almost six. His father was a moderately successful merchant. Spinoza grew up speaking Portuguese, Dutch and Hebrew, and proved to be one of the ablest young scholars in the Jewish schools. His elders expected him to become a great rabbi.

They were disappointed. In his early twenties, Spinoza began voicing serious doubts over the traditional concept of God, the afterlife and the veracity of the Bible. He was eventually excommunicated by the Jewish community in 1656, which meant that he was no longer free to live among its members, transact business with them, or come into any contact with them. Spinoza later claimed that the expulsion did not trouble him, since he had seen that such a break was inevitable. Besides, by this time his father had died (along with a sister, a brother and his stepmother), and he had no interest in continuing with the family business. Spinoza moved from Amsterdam, began calling himself "Benedict", and set up shop as a lens-grinder, pursuing at the same time his philosophical vision.

Spinoza soon found himself with a circle of philosophical friends and admirers who sought out his advice and his incisive intellect. He published a handbook of Descartes's philosophy, and circulated among his friends a couple of short treatises describing his own philosophical views. His reputation as a talented philosopher became known more broadly across Europe, although people who knew more details about his thought found it troubling and even heretical. In 1670 he published (anonymously, with a false place of publication) a treatise on theology and politics, which pointed out numerous flaws and inconsistencies in the Bible. It also defended a democratic republicanism, and a sweeping freedom to think what one pleases and to say what one thinks. The political topics were a pressing concern, since Spinoza was active in the attempt to preserve the Dutch republic from those who wanted the monarchy re-established. He was close friends with the DeWitt brothers, who championed the cause of republicanism, and who met grisly deaths at the hands of an angry mob.

This work, the *Theological-Political Treatise* (1670), scandalized its readers. Spinoza carefully dissected the first five books of the Bible and argued that they could not have been written by Moses, that they were written by various men of different temperaments, and that these temperaments led to very different portrayals of God, miracles and visions. He argued that the authors were ignorant and superstitious, although, for all that, they were able to discern and promote a decent moral code. He further argued that the best hope for civic order lies in curbing irrational belief and promoting reasonable discourse, and so the state should have no fear of granting philosophers the freedom to pursue the truths of reason.

It did not take long for readers to figure out who the author of this treatise was, since there were not many suspects who had so thorough a command of the Hebrew Bible, so penetrating a mind, so rebellious a spirit. But soon after this, Spinoza fell sick with tuberculosis, to which he succumbed in 1677, at the age of 44. Biographers who came looking for scandalous stories to tell of the "atheist Jew of Amsterdam" were surprised to discover that those who knew Spinoza knew him to be always fair, gentle and soft-spoken. He lived a moderate and quiet life, with many good friends, and in good relation to all his neighbours. He apparently never had any love interests and was tidy in all his business affairs. This puzzled many seventeenth-century Christians who could not imagine why someone would lead such an upright life without the fear of hell and hope of heaven before them. This, in a way, was the central lesson Spinoza wished to impart: that a virtuous life is its own reward.

The geometrical method

Spinoza is known mainly for his great work, the *Ethics*, which was in final form but unpublished at the time of his death. The *Ethics* is written in the style of Euclid's *Elements of Geometry*. It begins with definitions and axioms, and then proceeds to demonstrate proposition after proposition, with occasional scholia that drop in to provide some further explanation. The overall appearance is of a deductive fortress with each claim of Spinoza's philosophy cemented securely upon more fundamental ones, and the whole structure based upon solid axioms and definitions.

In reality the structure is not that solid (some commentators have gone so far as to charge that not a single demonstration of Spinoza's really works), but there is something to be learned from the way Spinoza delivers his philosophy. The *Ethics* seems to begin from a blank slate, as if we should not pretend to have any advanced knowledge of what is real. We have only some basic concepts, and our own rationality to see how these concepts are related to one another and what follows from them. Spinoza's strategy is to start with what reason tells us must be true, and to deduce whatever we can from these truths, regardless of whether our deductions fit with our ordinary experience. Again, as with Euclid, we are not to presume that we know anything beforehand. We are to let the axioms and definitions guide our way. And the final metaphysical vision Spinoza offers – namely, that the wild complexity of the world is in fact the expression of a single, timeless and unchanging substance – is surely one that appeals more to our reason than to our ordinary opinions.

That is only one reason Spinoza adopts a geometrical style. It is also clear that he thought this style was good pedagogy, since he used it as well in his handbook of Cartesian philosophy and in some letters to his friends meant to elucidate his thoughts. But of course Spinoza did not really just lay down some axioms he thought were true and then see what followed from them. He framed his axioms, and each proposition, with an eye towards the conclusions he wanted to establish, particularly those about the life of reason, the command of the passions, the advantages of democracy and the nature of moral life. His geometrical method is meant to display the overall connections among all these things. Even if the demonstrations are not as tight as Euclid's, they still offer to an impressive degree some insight into how all the elements in Spinoza's philosophy are supposed to fit together.

And, finally, perhaps Spinoza also thought the geometrical style was a metaphor for what he saw in the universe: a series of particular results flowing from a single source, with exactly the same necessity as it follows from the nature of a triangle that its angles are equal to two right angles. In other words, you and I and the events of our world follow from God with the same inevitable necessity as geometrical facts follow from the nature of space. All is necessary, and nothing could be otherwise.

Substance monism

The central claim of Spinoza's metaphysics is that there is only one substance, which can be called either "God" or "Nature". Everything else in the world – you, me, planets, candlesticks and butterflies – is a *mode* of God. As we shall see, this means that these things are not entirely distinct from God, but are instead finite ways in which God's attributes are expressed.

Before trying to understand what this means, we need to see Spinoza's argument for substance monism. Spinoza's argument draws upon three key ideas. First, he defines a "substance" as what is in itself and conceived through itself. For now, we should not try to have anything specific in mind as a substance, like a brick or a human or God or space. We should drop all previous associations, and allow Spinoza his definition: a substance is in itself and is conceived through itself. This means that a substance – *whatever* exactly it is – is wholly self-sufficient, both in its existence and in its conceivability. A substance requires no thing other than itself in order to exist or to be understood. So substances in general, as Spinoza understands them, can have no relation to one another. They do not cause one another, and we never need to have an understanding of one substance before gaining an understanding of another. Each of them is, in this sense, a world apart from the others.

Second, Spinoza defines an "attribute" as what the intellect conceives as essential to a substance. In order to help us understand this, we might recall that Descartes believed each substance to have a principal attribute. Bodies have the attribute of extension, and minds have the attribute of thought. Attributes are those features a thing cannot lose without going clean out of existence. They are essential to the thing. Similarly, Spinoza allowed his substances to have attributes or essences. But Spinoza, unlike Descartes, saw no reason to preclude a substance from having more than one attribute or essence. Descartes thought each substance has exactly one attribute; but since these attributes are conceptually distinct from one another, then it seems that no contradiction could be derived by supposing a substance to have several attributes. Being extended has no connection whatsoever with being thinking, for example. But if there is no connection between the two, there can be no contradiction in asserting that some substance has both attributes. Spinoza's substances can have several essences, each having absolutely nothing to do with the others – and though this may sound odd, or even bizarre, what contradiction could possibly be derived from such an arrangement?

So, all we know so far is that, first, substances are radically independent from one another, and, second, each has at least one attribute, and possibly many attributes. Third, Spinoza also demonstrates that substances (as he understands them) cannot possibly share any attributes (as he understands them). Why? Well, if they were to share an attribute, then they would share an essence. This would mean that they are *essentially* the same; and this would mean, Spinoza thinks, that they really are not distinct after all. In short, if A is essentially X, and B is essentially X, then A and B are essentially the same. But if they are essentially the same, then they are not distinct substances, on Spinoza's understanding of the term. We might see in this a criticism of Descartes's metaphysics. Descartes believed that minds share an attribute, and bodies share an attribute, but he never found an adequate way of individuating the things that share an attribute. Spinoza does not face this problem, since he simply lets substances that share an attribute be, in fact, one and the same substance. Thus, according to Spinoza, substances do not share attributes, or indeed *anything*, with one another. If they were to share anything, they would be the same.

With these three key ideas in place, we can now reveal Spinoza's argument for substance monism. He reaches his conclusion in three steps:

Step 1: It pertains to the nature of a substance to exist.

Spinoza reasons that a substance, as he defines the term, is wholly self-sufficient. It needs nothing other than itself in order to exist. So a substance does not need anything external to itself to bring it into existence. It has everything it needs completely on its own. So each substance, then, exists necessarily. (Certainly some objections can be raised here; but let us pursue the argument for now and see where it takes us.)

Step 2: The more essences (or attributes) a substance has, the greater its reality, or (in other words) its propensity to exist.

This step is difficult to explain, and our situation is not made easier by the fact that Spinoza, while relying on this step, does not offer any demonstration of it. This step is akin to the other rationalists' presumption that beings have various degrees of reality, or perfection (this was called the "gradations of reality thesis" in the introduction to this volume). Spinoza believes that substances' perfection – or their degree of reality – goes along with the number of their attributes. The more attributes, the greater the perfection, and the greater the reality. (It may be that this step was suggested to Spinoza by the language he was using: in Latin, the term "*esse*" signifies "essence" in its noun form and "exists" in its verb form. So it may have just seemed obvious to Spinoza that things with more "*esse*s" had more "*esse*".)

Step 3: Since substances cannot share attributes, and the ones with more essences have greater reality, there can in the end be only one substance – the one defined as having all possible attributes, which we call "God" or "Nature".

Thus Spinoza, in effect, argues for the necessary existence of all substances, but then allows the one with all the attributes to crowd the others out. A more accurate way of putting the idea is to say that the substance with the greatest perfection exists, and others exist only in so far as they are compatible with the first substance's existence. But since the most perfect substance has all possible attributes, no other substance is compatible with its existence. So there can be only one substance, the most perfect one, and it is God.

Spinoza defines "God" as the substance with infinite attributes, meaning all of them, but he never offers any ideas what attributes there might be in addition to thought and extension. Presumably he saw no reason why there should be only two attributes, or seventeen, or a million, and so concluded that there were endlessly many. And it is hard to think of an argument that demonstrates that thought and extension are the only possible attributes, even if they are the only two we can come up with. And Spinoza never sought an explanation for the fact that, although there may be infinite attributes, we can come up with only two.

Modes of the one substance

Spinoza lets his definitions and axioms lead him to the conclusion that there is only one substance. But at some point he has to connect that metaphysical conclusion with what we experience in our ordinary, human lives. If in truth there is just one substance, why do there seem to be so many separate things jostling about? Why is the world not awash in a single divine being?

All the things that seem different from God are *modes* of the one substance, says Spinoza. Modes, in contrast to substances, are entities that depend on other things for their existence and to be understood; they are "in" another and "conceived through" another. So all the things we experience are really "in" God, and "conceived through" God. And this fact makes them less "thinglike" on their own, and more dependent upon God for their existence.

What does this mean? Here interpreters of Spinoza disagree, but let us put forward one way of understanding Spinoza's central idea, and take up some alternative interpretations later. The traditional view of the relation between God and the world is that they are separate things. God made the world, and perhaps does something to keep it in existence, but it is properly understood as a separate "thing" in its own right. But according to Spinoza, the world and God are substantially the same: the world, and all the things in it, *are* God. Each thing is God in a different way: you are God in one way, I am God in another, and Mount Everest is God in yet a different way. But we are all God, fashioned in different ways. When we do things, it is God doing them – although God does them *in so far as* God is you, or me, or Mount Everest. The distinction between creator and creation collapses, or at least is made so narrow that we cannot distinguish God from creatures as individual things.

How does God, as the one substance, end up appearing as so many different things? To answer this question, we need to introduce some further details of Spinoza's metaphysics. Modes, according to Spinoza, come in two sizes: infinite and finite. The infinite modes of the one substance follow from the absolute nature of God's attributes. That is to say, God's essences immediately give rise to certain features of the world. Spinoza offers *motion and rest* as an example of an infinite mode following immediately from God's attribute of extension. So, given God's extension, there automatically follows motion and rest. From the absolute nature of God's attribute of thought – another attribute – there follows *infinite intellect*. From the point of view of

Spinoza's system, these infinite modes might be thought of as features or qualities that are "built into" the corresponding attributes: once there is extension, there must follow motion and rest, and once there is thought, there must follow infinite intellect. From our own point of view, we might conceive of these infinite modes as forces in nature. In the extended world there are universal forces of motion and rest; and in the world of thought, there is a universal force of logic, or reason.

Next: from these infinite modes there follow other infinite modes, such as (what Spinoza calls) "the face of the whole universe" – or the whole universe, conceived as a single entity. That is, given extension, and the forces of motion and rest, and given thought, and the force of reason – given all these attributes and infinite modes – there results our universe, as one infinite individual. And from this giant individual – finally! – there result all the smaller, finite parts of the individual: particular bodies and minds. One might envision Spinoza's universe as a single, great waterfall, which has an overall force and an overall roar and an overall wetness, and which tumbles out into a vast pool containing smaller eddies and currents and whirlpools. The roar and the wetness and the eddies and so on *just are* that big waterfall – but aspects of it or parts of it.

A full account of this great waterfall of all things flowing out from the abundance of God's nature is never given, and most of what Spinoza wrote on this topic is very obscure. The overall picture, at any rate, is that "From the necessity of the divine nature there must follow infinitely many things in infinitely many modes (i.e., everything which can fall under an infinite intellect)" (E 1p16). All existent things pile out of the divine nature automatically, with no act of will required on God's part.

Now it must be added that different interpreters have understood Spinoza's term "mode" in different ways. His earliest readers took him to mean that the finite things in our universe relate to God in the same way that properties (such as white, hard and round) are taken to relate to things (such as a ball of wax), since "mode" was commonly taken to refer to a kind of property. But it is hard to see how things like windmills and wooden shoes are anything like properties. (What would they be properties *of*?) Other readers have thought that by "mode" Spinoza meant to signify, not a property, but merely a thing that is not self-sufficient in the way that substances are. If so, then modes are just *things* that follow from the one substance. But then what exactly marks the independence of these things from the one substance? (In other words, what other than God are they supposed to be *made of*?)

But both accounts will agree that (as we have stressed) what is most important to keep in mind is that the things of this world are not *different in substance* from one another or from God. Each thing *is* God, modified in one way or another. Put in another way, each thing is a "way" (the literal meaning of the Latin term "*modus*") that God is expressed. Whether modes should be conceived as properties of God or as things that are by some measure distinguishable from God can be set aside as a topic for further debate.

Thus both the infinite and finite things in our universe follow from the one substance, according to Spinoza. The existence of these things and their behaviour are determined by the one substance. Thus Spinoza believes that all things are necessitated by God – "I have shown more clearly than the noon light that there is absolutely nothing in things on account of which they can be called contingent" (E 1p33s1). Spinoza is therefore a necessitarian: there is no sense in which things could be otherwise than they are. How a philosopher can believe this while at the same time recommending to his readers one form of life above the others is a puzzle we shall turn to in Chapter 4.

KEY POINTS

- According to Spinoza, there is only one substance in existence, call it "God" or "Nature". This one substance is completely self-sufficient and has all possible attributes or essences.
- The one substance has two attributes known by humans: thought and extension.
- The one substance has infinitely many "modes", or "ways" in which the attributes of the one substance are expressed.
- Each thing in the universe is a mode of God.

Spinoza's God

From this it is clear that Spinoza's God is not the same sort of divine being worshipped by theists. We can see why he thought "Nature" might be a better word for what he had in mind. Spinoza's God does not decide to create things; instead, things flow or emanate from the one substance. Praying to Spinoza's God would be useless, as this God cannot act in any other way; it would be like praying to gravity, or electromagnetism. And as Spinoza goes on to argue, none of the features we associate with persons, such as desires and hopes and fears, have any place in relation to God. Spinoza's God or Nature is a great, cosmic, impersonal force, bringing about consequences with the same dispassion as a mechanical algorithm, and this force is neither disappointed nor cheered by anything that gets cranked out. Everything is equally natural, so far as Nature is concerned – a pile of stones, a pile of bodies, it matters not. Only humans (and some other animals) come to prefer some outcomes to others.

Spinoza's outlook may thus feel extremely cold. It certainly did to many of his early readers. He understands that most of us want nothing more than some reassurance that we are valuable; that our lives matter; that there is some plan for us and concern for us. But he thinks we should not expect to find these things outside the concern we have for ourselves and one another. We are big enough, Spinoza might say, to live on our own, and get out from under the idea of some Great Father looking out for us. We need to unmask traditional religion for the superstition it is, and trust science and reason to tell us what the world is really like, and how we ought to live in order to flourish as natural beings.

Still, although Spinoza wanted to dispel the notion of a warm, caring father figure, he did have definite roles for his God or Nature to play. His one substance is meant to bring true *unity* into the universe, with respect to both its structure and our knowledge of it. Descartes had split the universe into a realm of thought and a realm of extension, and he was never fully able to reunite the two into a single structure. The fundamental tenet of Spinoza's metaphysics, in contrast, is that *all of reality is one*, although that one thing may come to be "expressed" as extended or thinking or whatever. Only the truth of *some* kind of monism allows for the possibility of a truly unified body of knowledge. If the world were dualistic, then the best we could attain would be a conjunction of two theories, neither reducible to the other. And while any full understanding of the whole world would be a welcome achievement, there is clearly greater satisfaction in having one theory that binds everything together rather than two or more. Later, as the nineteenth-century German idealists began building vast philosophical systems that were as broad as they were deep, they found Spinoza to be a great source of inspiration.

Parallelism

Spinoza's God consists of "infinite" attributes – thought, extension and anything else. (Spinoza writes as if the list could be continued without end, but admits that he can conceive of only these two.) But there is just one substance. So Spinoza concludes that the modes of this one substance are like God in having all possible attributes – each mode is thinking, and extended and whatever else. That is, each mode can be fully understood as a thinking thing, or as an extended thing, and so on. Spinoza's way of putting it is that "The order and connection of ideas is the same as the order and connection of things" (E 2p7). In this way, the unity Spinoza sees in nature extends into each individual thing.

In the case of human beings, this parallelism is meant to explain the apparent duality of mind and body. As Descartes knew, mind and body seem totally distinct from one another. But since, according to Spinoza, a single thing can have multiple attributes, there is no reason to suppose that mind and body are not the same thing, conceived under different attributes: the human being considered under the attribute of thought is a mind, and the same human being considered under the attribute of extension is a body. Spinoza could have used analytic geometry as an analogy to explain this dual-aspect theory. An algebraic formula and a geometrical curve may express the very same mathematical relationship; the relationship can be considered under the "attribute" of algebra or under the "attribute" of geometry. Similarly, the same entity, in Spinoza's metaphysics, can be understood as either a body or a mind (or an idea).

In fact – as surprising as it may sound, at first – most of us ordinarily view ourselves in this way. We know that our brains have a lot to do with our consciousness, and we slide easily from talking about our brains to talking about our minds. But we can also recognize a deep difference between the two. We can know what is going on in our minds just by reflecting, and cannot know what is happening in our brains without surgery or special scanning equipment. We know one "from being on the inside", and know the other only "by looking from the outside". It is as if the brain and mind are accessible through two different dimensions, a mental one and a physical one, although we believe at the same time that they are somehow one and the same thing. This is Spinoza's view.

Now Spinoza extends this view not just to humans, but to all finite modes whatsoever. So each and every thing has both (or, better, *is* both) a body and a mind. But this does not mean that each thing in the universe is conscious in the way a human is conscious. A thing's mind is only as complex as its body is: in so far as a body is capable of complex interactions with its environment, the mind also can have complex relations with its environment. A stone is capable of very little interaction, so its "mind" is quite simple. But human bodies are capable of perceiving many things and causing many things, so their minds are quite complex. This *panpsychism* ("souls everywhere") of Spinoza is an important part of his thesis that humans are not especially unique in nature. Each thing has some degree of mentality, and although humans have a lot of it, this does not make them different in kind from other creatures. Indeed, somewhere in the universe there probably are bodies much more complex than human bodies, with minds that are greater than our own. The universe in its entirety, as we shall see, is one such body – the body of God – with a corresponding mind that could well be called the mind of God.

Spinoza identifies each thing's mind with the *idea* of its body. This makes it easy to accept the thesis that everything has a mind, since for each body we can form the idea of that body. But it is not clear that the ideas we form are what we would ordinarily think of as minds. When I form an idea of a mill, I think of the function, operation and fundamental components of a mill. This representation, if accurate, captures what a mill is and what it does. But in what sense is it a *mind*? In forming the idea of a mill in my mind, do I thereby introduce the mind of the mill into my own? How does an idea of a thing have any degree of consciousness?

We can go some way towards answering these questions by thinking of minds in Spinoza's philosophy as collections of "living" ideas, each striving to continue in existence just as bodies do. So think of a field of ideas. Each idea contains within itself some degree of clarity and distinctness; ideas are related to one another in terms of logical consequence, cause and effect; some ideas are more powerful than others and can supplant them. A complex of such ideas, with appropriate relations among them, constitutes a mind, just as a system of organs composes a larger body. Perhaps, with such a view, the difference between what we typically recognize as a mind and what we typically think of as a mere idea is only a difference in degree – a difference in the complexity among each thing's parts.

Spinoza did not work out any of this in detail, and it is hard to believe that his purpose in asserting that minds are ideas of bodies was to provide a compelling account of consciousness. He was not trying to solve that problem. Probably he made the identification because he found that it is a neat way to form a one-to-one correspondence between all the bodies and all the minds.

An analogy, and a question

In part 2 of the *Ethics*, Spinoza offers a geometrical analogy for his substance monism combined with his parallelism, and it is an analogy worth studying. The analogy concerns a result Euclid proves about lines that intersect within a circle. Begin with a circle, and draw two lines that intersect anywhere within that circle. Now break each of those lines into the parts marked by the intersection, and use them to construct two rectangles, one from the parts of one line, and the other from the parts of the other line. Euclid proves that the two rectangles thus formed will have the same area. This is surprising, but true. The relation holds for the infinitely many intersecting lines within any given circle.

Spinoza thinks this is analogous to his own philosophy. Just as the circle "contains" (or offers the possibility of) infinitely many intersecting lines, God or Nature contains infinitely many modes. And just as, for each pair of intersecting lines, there are two different rectangles "expressing" the same area, Spinoza claims that for each mode, there is that mode expressed as an extended thing and that same mode expressed as a thinking thing. Moreover, this analogy illustrates the claim that Spinoza frequently makes, that all things are contained in God in just the same way that, for example, a triangle "contains" the fact that its angles are equal to two right angles. Things follow from God with geometrical necessity, and each thing is as necessary and unavoidable as a mathematical fact.

But this analogy also leads to a deep and difficult question about Spinoza's monism. We have seen that Spinoza thinks all modes are somehow "contained" in God, and that they are necessitated by God. The question is whether Spinoza believes there are any "unactualized" possibles – that is, things that are conceivable without contradiction, but never as a matter of fact come to exist in the universe (such as unicorns, perhaps, or leprechauns, or a thousand-and-one-sided chunk of lead). On the one hand, it seems that Spinoza should say there are no unactualized possibles; for how could any of them be genuinely possible, if they do not flow automatically from the nature of Spinoza's God? In what sense could they *possibly* come about? In further support of this, Spinoza does claim that God brings about everything that is in God's infinite intellect, and so it seems that everything possible does come to be actual. But, on the other hand, in the very same place where he offers the circle-and-lines analogy, Spinoza writes of "singular things that do not exist", which are contained in God's nature in just the same way as the singular things that do exist. And in other places Spinoza writes of pure and perfect geometrical objects which we can reason about, even if it just so happens that none of them ever come to actually exist.

There seem to be three ways of understanding what Spinoza believes about unactualized possibles. First, perhaps Spinoza means that they are conceivable without contradiction, but they simply never get the "chance" to exist, because they get shouldered out by all the other things that come to exist. Since these other things are necessitated by God, we can truly say that these conceivable things are not truly possible, though they are conceivable without contradiction. Or, second, Spinoza could say that these allegedly conceivable things really are not conceivable, once we have a proper understanding of what God's intellect includes. We might think a unicorn or a leprechaun or a thousand-and-one-sided figure is conceivable, but perhaps it really is not, once we understand more about God's nature. Or, finally, Spinoza could believe that all of these conceivable things really do come to exist sometime, somewhere in our universe, and passages that appear to say otherwise are either mistaken or need to be interpreted in some other way.

A further complication about necessity

There is an additional complication to be noted as well. Earlier, in describing the modes of the one substance, it was said that each one's existence and behaviour is determined by the one substance. But in fact Spinoza demonstrates that an individual finite mode, such as a lamp, is not brought into existence simply out of God's pure nature. Instead, it is brought into existence by that nature, along with the causal forces of other finite modes – the metal, the oil, the efforts of the lamp's maker, the design, and so on. All things taken together (God along with these finite modes of God) make the existence of the lamp and its behaviour necessary. So it is wrong to say that all things are necessitated by God's nature; it is more accurate to say that all things are necessitated by God's nature, together with other, already-existent finite modes. God, plus the things existing in the world, necessitate what comes into existence.

This picture should be familiar enough, as any determinist believes that events are determined by the laws of nature, in conjunction with their antecedent causes. (The laws of combustion, together with the presence of a spark and dynamite, determine the explosion.) Spinoza is saying something similar when he claims that the nature of the one substance, in conjunction with the already-existent modes, determines the existence of subsequent modes. But this familiar picture raises a further question: where do finite modes come from in the first place? If, in order to produce one, you need an already-existent one, then how does the whole sequence of finite modes get started?

Spinoza's first answer is "*ad infinitum*". In other words, there was no first finite mode in time; the age of the world is infinite. Still, though, we will ask, why are there any finite modes at all? Is there an explanation for the existence of finite modes in general?

Spinoza does not answer this question directly, but here are two possible replies he could make. First, he could point out that the existence of each and every finite mode has been explained, and that is enough. By accounting for the existence of each and every finite mode, he has accounted for the existence of all finite modes. It is just that he does not have a *single* explanation for the totality of finite modes. He has, instead, a different explanation for each one. That perhaps is not as unified an explanation as one might expect from a rationalist, but perhaps no such unified explanation exists. Spinoza's second possible reply is to say that the totality of finite modes, the total collection of all finite individuals in the universe, is itself an infinite mode of God – the "face of the whole universe", as he calls it in a letter to a friend. As an infinite mode, it *does* follow from the absolute nature of God's attributes. Thus if we want an explanation for the existence of finite modes in general, we shall find that their totality is indeed necessitated by God's nature. If we want an explanation for the existence of individual finite modes, however, we shall need to appeal to both God's nature and already-existent finite modes. So far, so good. But the problem with this second reply is that it is hard to see why we should have to appeal to already-existent finite modes when trying to account for the existence of an individual mode, if the totality of finite modes is already necessitated by God's nature. Has each finite mode not already been necessitated by God's nature? If so, then why not say that each and every finite mode is necessitated by God's nature? Yet Spinoza explicitly denies that this is so.

> **KEY POINTS**
>
> - All things follow from God or Nature in some way or other. Infinite modes follow from God's nature. Finite modes follow from that nature, in conjunction with other, already-existent finite modes. In the end, all things owe their existence to the one substance.
> - God, as the one substance, is both thinking and extended. Each individual mode is also both thinking and extended.
> - The human being, as an extended thing, is a body, and that same being, as a thinking thing, is a mind. Mind and body are the same thing, conceived in two different ways.
> - What is said of the human being on this matter can be said as well of any finite mode. This view, that all things have a mind in at least some degree, is called "panpsychism".

God's extension

Spinoza is radical in his claim that extension is an attribute of God – that is, that God is an extended thing. Most thinkers deny that God is extended for a couple of reasons. First, extended things can be acted upon, but God is wholly active and never passive; and, second, extended things can be divided and destroyed, but God cannot. But Spinoza reverses the argument: *since* we know God is extended, we can therefore conclude that not all extended things are purely passive, and not all extended things are divisible.

The key to Spinoza's denial of God's divisibility is the way he thinks of matter and extension. Like Descartes, he thinks of extension as an attribute or a property, so he does not think there can be any extension without *something* having the property of being extended. So the upshot is that there can be no vacua – no empty spaces. What seem to us like empty spaces are in fact filled with very fine or light matter. Now if we think of God's extension as the entire universe of matter, the claim that God is indivisible, according to Spinoza, amounts to the claim that there is no way to separate or break apart matter without still having matter between the parts. In other words, if you want to divide matter into two pieces, you will have to insert some immaterial extended thing between the two pieces. But there are no immaterial extended things. So you cannot divide matter. So God, as the one extended substance, cannot be divided, QED.

But modes of the one substance can be divided. That is, you can divide a stone into two pieces by inserting something that is not stone between them (such as air, water, a metal blade, and so on). Thus stone *in so far as it is stone* is divisible, but stone *in so far as it is matter* (or *extended*) is not divisible. This leads us to a question about Spinoza's account of bodies: what exactly makes one hunk of matter stone, and another hunk of matter something other than stone?

This is connected with the problem of individuating bodies, which we saw in relation to Descartes's physics. The solution to the problem, according to Spinoza, must be given solely in terms of motion, which is the infinite mode of extension. So stone is distinguished from water on the basis of the motions of their parts. We might conceive of a stone as a certain kind of stable "swirl" of matter – a swirl that results in the stone's properties of being hard and heavy. And a pool of water is a different kind of swirl of matter, one that gives rise to the water's properties of being fluid and drinkable. Spinoza calls these swirls "patterns of motion and rest" among the constituent parts of the bodies. Each body is a certain pattern of motion and rest, and each body strives to maintain that pattern over time. These strivings of bodies to maintain themselves are the essences of those bodies, according to Spinoza; ultimately, these different strivings make bodies distinct from one another.

Thus Spinoza's big picture of the physical universe is of an infinite sea of matter, with infinitely many stable, swirling patterns, which are the individual bodies in the universe. But these bodies are also arranged in a kind of vertical hierarchy, from the simplest to the most complex. Spinoza writes of simplest bodies, which have no internal complexity, and move as wholes from one location to another. These simplest bodies swirl together in stable patterns to form complex bodies. These complex bodies form even more complex bodies. And these form even greater complex bodies, and so on, until we reach the universe as a whole, which is one great big body, "whose parts, that is, all bodies, vary in infinite ways, without any change of the whole individual" (E 2L7s). The universe of bodies is a body itself, and strives to maintain its own stable pattern of motion and rest.

In striving to maintain itself, the universe as a whole must determine the motions of its parts. That is, for every acceleration in one part of the universe, there must be a corresponding deceleration elsewhere, so that the overall pattern is kept stable. The universe, in a sense, keeps its own metabolism. And the forces with which the universe maintains its own metabolism are the forces of nature, described by the laws of nature. In a letter to a correspondent, Spinoza compares our situation in the universe to that of a worm living in someone's blood. The little worm sees all kinds of motions within the body, but does not realize that all of these motions result from the body's striving to maintain its health and temperature. Similarly, we see motions in the universe, but do not recognize that all of these motions are the ways by which the universe maintains itself as an individual.

Determination of the will

Just as all bodily motions are determined by other bodies and the broad causal forces of the universe, Spinoza thinks that ideas are determined by other ideas and the laws of thought. His doctrine of parallelism commits him to this view, since the order and connection of ideas is the same as the order and connection of bodies. When a system of bodies is in a certain state at a certain time, the laws of nature will determine the next state for the system; and that determines the next, and so on. Similarly, when a system of ideas (a mind) is in a certain state, the laws of thought will determine the next state of that mind. Spinoza never explains exactly what these laws of thought might be, other than saying (as by now we should come to expect) that the laws of thought will be the same as the laws of extension, expressed under a different attribute.

So the sequence of our thoughts is just as determined as a sequence of collisions among bodies: one thought determines the next, which determines the next, and so on. We do not have the freedom to direct our thoughts so that we may choose to think first of one thing, and then another. Of course, it *seems* to us as if we do, but Spinoza would say that this is merely because we are not aware of all of the forces determining our thoughts. Try imagining a pink elephant. Now reflect: was the elephant facing you, or turned to the right, or to the left? Did you choose to imagine it that way, or did that way of imagining it simply "pop" into your mind, determined by forces outside your own awareness? As Spinoza writes, many people say that human actions and thoughts depend on the will, but

> these are only words for which they have no idea. For all are ignorant of what the will is, and how it moves the Body; those who boast of something else, who feign seats and dwelling places of the soul, usually provoke either ridicule or disgust.
> (E 2p35s)

On this matter, as on others, Spinoza clearly disagrees with Descartes. Our thoughts, he thinks, are just as determined as bodies in motion.

Now this might seem to pose a problem for the advice Spinoza wishes to give, both on moral matters and on the subject of trying to gain a clearer picture of reality. What use is this advice if the sequence of our thoughts is rigidly determined? In reply, Spinoza might say that when he seems to be giving advice, he is only observing what happens from time to time – for example, "when people do thus-and-so, they end up being happier", and "when illusion gets replaced by knowledge, people are better equipped to respond to the world". He need not suppose that anyone is able to act upon these observations in order for these observations to be true. Spinoza might also observe that, in writing the *Ethics*, he is complicating the chains of causes that bring us to do what we do and think what we think. And so we might end up behaving morally and gaining adequate ideas *precisely because* Spinoza's words exerted causal influences upon us!

Spinoza further argues that there is no separate component of the mind whose task it is to affirm or deny the ideas that we entertain. In other words, there is no will. We should recall that Descartes believed that the intellect is distinct from the will; and it is because the intellect can conceive only so much, and the will can affirm or deny anything, that we make mistakes in our judgements. In contrast, Spinoza believes that whenever we entertain an idea, the idea has built into it some degree of affirmation; in conceiving the idea, we are drawn to affirm the existence of the object, to some degree. For example, in conceiving a winged horse, we conceive of what seems to us to be a possible thing. (It certainly seems more possible than a contemplative brick, let alone a round square.) As our conception gets increasingly detailed – a winged horse in ancient Persia, belonging to Xerxes, and so on – we affirm more and more in our conception. In the limit, if we have conceived of a thing with perfect adequacy, we have affirmed the existence of a real thing. In this example of a winged horse, presumably we will encounter some obstacle in conceiving it adequately – some conflict perhaps with other things we know to be true – if indeed it is true that Pegasus never existed.

Two further notes must be made about this claim. First, Spinoza explicitly claims that there is some degree of truth or reality in every idea. There are elements of truth in our idea of Santa Claus, for instance – there are reindeer, and things that fly, and there is a North Pole, and we do encounter jolly and generous fellows. But not every aspect of our idea of Santa Claus is fully thought out (as we discover at all too tender an age). The only idea with absolutely no element of truth is the idea of a straightforwardly contradictory thing, such as a nephew whose parents have no siblings. So one might say that the "reality" of an idea goes along with the intelligibility of its content: the more conceivable a thing is, the more real it is. The second note is that it seems to follow that, on Spinoza's account, there cannot be a perfectly adequate idea of a nonexistent or unreal thing – to be adequately conceived is to be real. If something can be understood, then it is real: "No truly sound reason can persuade us to believe that God did not will to create all the things which are in his intellect, with that same perfection with which he understands them" (E 1p33s2). Referring back to our previous discussion of the circle-and-lines analogy, this consequence lends support to believing that when Spinoza says that nothing could be otherwise, he means that every conceivable thing becomes actual sometime.

Knowledge

Spinoza thinks there are three ways in which we gain beliefs or knowledge: through casual experience, through reason and through intuition.

The first kind of knowledge, through casual experience, accounts for the bulk of the beliefs we have about the world. We read things, or see things, or hear things, and as a result, we build up an internal model of the outside world – the world according to our casual (or unstructured) experience. It is important to remember that, according to Spinoza, the mental construction of a model of our world is paralleled by some set of physical transformations in our body or brain. We see an event, and the light entering our eyes causes changes in our nerves and brains so that some information is recorded. That physical record, conceived under the attribute of thought, is our memory of the event. But this memory, Spinoza argues, is as much about the physiological state of our body as it is about the event: it is a "picture" of the event, but at the same time a picture of the body recording that event. All sensory experiences are mediated by our bodily states in this way. For this reason, the ideas we gain through casual experience are usually inadequate representations of things – they are literally "con-fusions" in which our bodily states are fused together with some purported representation of things outside our body. This first kind of "knowledge", then, is more accurately called a way in which we form *beliefs* – beliefs that may or may not match up with what is really going on in the world.

The second kind of knowledge is through rational demonstrations. Just as there are features all bodies have in common – such as size, shape and motion – Spinoza thinks there are features all minds have in common, which are the ideas of the features all bodies have in common. Spinoza calls these basic ideas *common notions*, and they are surely meant to include all the ideas we require in order to build up a complete account of what is real. Because we have ideas of size, shape and motion (and others), we are able to construct an adequate model of the world, one that can take the place of the inadequate one we build up through casual experience. The common notions are innate to the mind – they are innate to *all* minds. And when we have built up an explanation or account of something through our common notions, there is an important sense in which our knowledge has been built up *autonomously*, or from our own resources – as opposed to the first kind of knowledge, where our thinking is determined by causal interaction with bodies external to our own.

The first and second kinds of knowledge can be contrasted with an example. We see two cars collide. If we have watched correctly, and if we also listen to other witnesses' reports, we can build up an account of the crash. This would be knowledge of the first kind. But suppose we are not satisfied with this, and we want to know the masses of the cars, and their velocities and so on. We take our measurements, pull out our clipboards and our physics textbooks, and begin to develop an account of the crash that is both more abstract and more accurate. We draw upon the basic forces and qualities that affect all bodies, and forget about irrelevant features such as the colours of the cars or the smell of burning rubber. This would be the second kind of knowledge, which is rooted in key concepts of physics and mathematics instead of merely the sensations we happened to receive. And if the second account conflicts with what we think we saw, and we are sure we have done our measuring and our mathematics correctly, we will discount what we saw in favour of what reason tells us. For the senses can deceive; physics cannot.

The third kind of knowledge is harder to understand. Spinoza calls it *intuitive knowledge*, and describes it as knowledge "which proceeds from an adequate idea of the formal essence of certain attributes of God to the adequate knowledge of the essence of things" (E 2p40s2). It is a kind of direct insight. Spinoza's example of this kind of knowledge is seeing "in one glance" that 1 is to 2 as 3 is to 6. We do not need to see if this coheres with the rules we have been taught about calculating proportions, and we do not need to demonstrate its truth – we just *see* that these pairs of numbers have the same proportion. This example is fairly humdrum, but by the end of the *Ethics* Spinoza claims that this kind of knowledge enables us to see things' inner connection with the nature of God, and that this knowledge brings our minds the greatest possible joy, which he identifies as "the intellectual love of God". Perhaps Spinoza means to say that, in virtue of all things being united in God, one part can come to have immediate knowledge of other parts, in a kind of mystical union our mind can have with the objects of its knowledge. (That would explain Spinoza's apparent enthusiasm over this type of knowledge; he calls it our highest blessedness.) Or perhaps Spinoza is claiming simply that our mind is able to perceive some elementary truths directly. (And then his apparent enthusiasm is perhaps an attempt to say the sorts of things religious people say but mean something much more down to earth – a kind of "double-speak.") Spinoza does not say enough about the third kind of knowledge for us to be sure what he meant.

It is worth remarking that this third kind of knowledge seems to play a different role in Spinoza's philosophy than the natural light does in Descartes's. Descartes used the natural light to secure basic epistemological and metaphysical principles such as the *cogito* and the causal adequacy principle. But Spinoza uses the common notions for the purpose of securing fundamental principles. The third kind of knowledge is something beyond that. It provides us with immediate certainty of truths that are themselves demonstrable through the second kind of knowledge, but in a kind of direct intellectual perception that brings the mind its highest joy.

KEY POINTS

- Finite bodies maintain a stable pattern of motion or activity over time, and so does the universe as a whole. Spinoza's model of the universe is organic: we are living things, within a larger living thing, like a tiny animal in a larger host's bloodstream.
- The mind is thoroughly determined, as are our desires, decisions and actions.
- We come to know the world through casual sensory experience (which is always to some degree confused), or through rational demonstrations based on common notions, or through a special kind of direct intellectual insight.

Key points

- There is one substance in existence, according to Spinoza. He calls this substance "God", but it is unlike traditional notions of God. It is an impersonal force that is causally responsible for generating our universe.
- All things are necessitated by this one substance. Human thought and behaviour are rigidly determined: nothing can be otherwise.
- We can gain knowledge of the one substance, and of things in the universe, through the employment of reason.
- We can come to intuit necessary features of the universe through a special kind of knowledge, which brings the mind its greatest joy.

four

Spinoza's ethics, politics and religion

Lines, planes and bodies

In the preface to part 3 of the *Ethics*, Spinoza writes that he intended to consider human actions and appetites "just as if it were a question of lines, planes, and bodies". He intends to provide a geometry of the emotions, that is, a scientific or even mechanical account of why humans do what they do and feel what they feel. What he wrote is meant primarily as an explanation for what actually happens, although at the same time Spinoza manages to give some advice about what humans should do if they want to have the best chances of experiencing more satisfaction than misery in their lives.

It should be observed at the outset that Spinoza is not very optimistic about our chances of success. Human beings are relatively weak finite modes of the one substance; there are many natural forces – from earthquakes and avalanches to viruses and strokes – that can overwhelm us, diminish us and destroy us. It is a certainty that eventually we will be worn down by the world, die and disintegrate. Along the way we will find that "we are driven about in many ways by external causes, and that, like waves upon the sea, driven by contrary winds, we toss about, not knowing our outcome and fate" (E 3p59s). Still, as we shall see, Spinoza does think there is a way of life that we would be wise to pursue, even if there is no doubt about our vulnerability and our eventual failure. His advice is to live as *autonomously* as possible – that is, to be as self-governed and self-determined as the nature of things will permit. To the extent we succeed, we shall experience greater power over our lives, and greater joy.

Physiology and psychology

Any body, according to Spinoza, is a mode of God's extension, meaning that it is a particular way in which God's extension is expressed. In the case of human bodies, extension is expressed in a complex way. The body is composed of numerous organs, all sensitively attuned to one another so that as a whole they make a single organic life. If that attunement is severely disrupted – by a bullet, or an illness, or the ravages of a mob – then the organism dies. Lesser damages will impair its functioning in some way or other, and the body will try to repair those damages and restore itself to health. Bodies strive towards health, and towards increased power, so that they will be able to withstand attacks for as long as possible. A thing's striving towards its own preservation is called its *conatus* ("striving"), which Spinoza identifies as the actual essence of a thing.

We know from Spinoza's doctrine of parallelism that whatever is said of the body must be said in an analogous way of the idea or mind of that body. So the mind also is a complex entity, according to Spinoza, composed of ideas in the same way that a body is composed of organs. Indeed, since the human mind is the idea of the body, there will be ideas in the mind of everything going on in the body, from processes of digestion to impacts upon the sense organs. And just as the body is sensitive to ways in which the environment will affect it, so too is the mind sensitive to ideas that come to it from outside sources. These ideas are called *affects*, or passions, and according to Spinoza they are always inadequate. Whenever an idea comes to us from outside – say from a gaudy billboard or from some lecturer haranguing us about one thing or another – the idea will be a confusion of two things: what is going on outside us, and what is going on inside us as we receive these impressions and process them. As we saw in connection with Spinoza's account of knowledge, input from the outside world will always give us inadequate ideas.

The only adequate ideas we have are the ones built from ideas that are innate to the mind – the common notions. Our minds strive to build adequate ideas from common notions, and attain adequate knowledge of our world, in the same way that our bodies try to maintain their health. If the body's *conatus* is to preserve itself and grow in strength, then the mind's *conatus* is to preserve itself and grow in knowledge. The body wants to drive itself, so to speak, and insulate itself from environmental threats, and the mind also wants to determine its own thinking from its own ideas.

The big psychological battle of our lives, according to Spinoza, is a battle for *autonomy*, or "self-rule". To the extent that our actions and thoughts are due to the strivings of our bodies and minds, we shall preserve ourselves and grow in strength. Self-determination, according to Spinoza, is freedom – though not, of course, freedom in the sense of being able to do otherwise than we do. Remember that the nature of the one substance necessitates all things; nothing can be otherwise. Instead, it is freedom in the sense of being *free from* outside influences or coercion. It is the freedom of doing exactly what it is you want to do – or, to be more accurate, to do exactly as your actual essence wants you to do.

The bad news is that we will lose this battle. Just as our bodies will end up craving tobacco or alcohol or potato chips, our minds will end up craving outside stimulation and ideas that really do not build up our own mental autonomy. Human lives, on the whole, are polluted by outside sources, and so the bulk of humanity eagerly chases after its own demise. We do not do this knowingly, of course. We all try to do what is in our own best interest. But we get funny ideas of what our best interest is, especially since so many of the ideas we have are inadequate. We taste those snacks, and we experience some pleasure, and it is true that some of the ingredients in the snacks have some healthful features. So we eat more and more of them, gaining more and more pleasure, without recognizing the long-term consequences of the other, less healthy features of the snacks. Or, similarly, we succumb to superstitious ideas, since there always seems to be some rationale for them, and we do not perceive the ways in which they fall short of an adequate understanding of things. Spinoza's diagnosis of our difficult situation should be familiar: the world is not always as it appears, and since we do not know any better, we end up ingesting foods and notions that in the long run will do us more harm than good.

The free man

How would our lives be different if we were perfectly free? – if our lives were governed entirely by our inner resources? Spinoza discusses such a life in part 4 of the *Ethics*, and constructs the ideal "free man" to serve as an "exemplar" for us – a kind of philosophical hero we should try to emulate, at least so far as we can.

"The free man", writes Spinoza, "thinks of nothing less than death, and his wisdom is a meditation on life, not on death" (E 4p67). This is Spinoza's first remark about the free man, and it is an important observation. Our actual essence is a striving for life and for power, and a striving towards adequate knowledge. In this sense it is wholly positive – wholly aggressive, in other words, in the cause of our own interest. Spinoza's English predecessor, Thomas Hobbes (1588–1679), placed in the essence of each human being "a striving for power after power which ceaseth only in death", and Spinoza does the same. The free man is obsessed with life, power and knowledge, and never falls into any sort of morose despair. The free man is hungry for more life, both physically and mentally, and eagerly consumes as much as he is able.

Moreover, the free man has no concept of good and evil – only "what is good for me" and "what impedes my growth". Of course, nothing in Spinoza's universe is inherently good or evil; the universe is perfectly value-free and neutral. We are the ones who regard things as good or evil, in so far as they help us or hinder us. Spinoza's free man does whatever he can to escape or avoid any threats to his own self-determination and growth, and he avoids contact with ignorant fellows, since they may do foolish things that might impede his own flourishing. In that sense, he regards them as "evil". He does not hate these ignorant people; he simply regards them as lesser beings, in a way, likely to bring him more trouble than benefit. He is grateful to other free men, since he can trust them to work cooperatively with him so that they may all enjoy the rewards of their combined efforts. (Thus they are "good".) The free man, in short, distances himself from the rabble, and pursues his own advantage, trusting only his fellow free men to aid him in the pursuit of his own power and self-determination. To the extent that we can do this, Spinoza thinks, we will be *virtuous*.

So that is how we would be if we were completely free, according to Spinoza. The exemplar may seem unfamiliar to us, or undesirable: is this how we really want to be, deep down? We might feel that this role model is a selfish and amoral snob. But Spinoza might respond that we feel this way only because we have not learned the lessons of part 1 of the *Ethics*. The universe (or "God") *does not care*, he might remind us; nature churns out results without any thought as to what we might want or need. All of nature is nothing but finite modes trying to preserve themselves, and human beings are no exceptions. *See things as they are,* he might advise, *and not as you wish them to be; remove your blinkers, your primitive mythologies, and all those childish things you say you learned in kindergarten. The truly free man has no use for them.*

It is for this reason that Friedrich Nietzsche, the nineteenth-century German philosopher, was so excited when he first read Spinoza. He found in Spinoza just the same cold and hard aloofness he would later build into his concept of the philosophical superman. Nietzsche argued that we must regard the old God as dead, and step beyond the concepts of good and evil, and "become who we are" – namely, selfish and amoral snobs. Spinoza had reached these rather frightening conclusions as early as the seventeenth century.

Of human bondage

We should remember that Spinoza is not telling us that we should try to adopt the qualities of the free man, as if we were now anything else. We *are* the free man, deep down, beneath all our other qualities. The free man is just the full expression of our actual essence. So what exactly keeps us from attaining this full expression? What is holding us back?

In a word, we are held back by our *bondage* to inadequate ideas or passions. Spinoza offers a detailed account of human passions, how they are caused, and how they control our lives. We shall review this account so that we get a better idea of the task that lies before us, according to Spinoza.

Spinoza builds his account of human passions on three basic experiences: *joy*, which we feel when we gain power; *sorrow*, which we feel when we lose power; and *desire*, which is our inherent striving to preserve ourselves and grow in power. All of our passions are based on these three, and Spinoza devotes part 3 of the *Ethics* to describing exactly how. Love, for example, is the experience of joy, conjoined with the idea of something as the cause of that joy, and hate is the experience of sadness, conjoined with the idea of something as the cause of that sadness. We experience hope when we have the idea of an event that will bring us joy, but we are not sure that the event will come about, and fear is what we feel when the event we imagine will bring us sadness. Confidence, despair, pride, remorse, lust and pity are all defined in similar ways, out of the emotions previously constructed. Spinoza makes good on his promise to provide a geometry of the passions, constructing more than *forty* of them from the basic elements, as if armed with a compass and straightedge. (Spinoza's account of the passions is much like the one offered by Descartes in *The Passions of the Soul*, although there are interesting differences of detail.)

If somehow we could guarantee that when we felt love or hate, it was directed at an object that brought us true joy or sorrow, we would not experience bondage to the passions. We would love and hate only the things we really should love and hate. But the main problem is that we get confused about what brings us joy and sadness. So, for example, a lovely person comes along and makes us feel good about what we are doing, and we feel joy, and think of that person as the cause of our joy. So we fall madly in love with that person, and experience jealousy over anyone else who receives his attention. We feel longing for him when he is absent, and even despair when we find that he is not returning our phone calls. If we had only recognized at the beginning that this person was not the cause of our joy, so much as the ideas he caused in us which promoted our own self-esteem, which is itself a very great joy for us! Then we would have loved what was said, not who said it, and would have avoided great anguish. We are finite and limited, and the world often confuses us about what causes what. Hence our bondage.

Spinoza thus follows Plato in believing that all (or much) of our suffering arises from failures to know. If we could restrain ourselves from acting on inadequate ideas, then our emotions would be as well ordered as our intellects. But we are parts of nature that cannot help but form inadequate ideas and act on them. The free man is a mirage of sorts, a finite thing that is never bested by more powerful things. Still, we can try to restrain ourselves as much as possible, and try to align our emotions with our intellects – this is Spinoza's general prescription for our troubles.

Passions, by themselves, are neither good nor evil, of course. They come about necessarily, given how we are and what our experiences are. Still, it can be seen that many of them impede our striving for self-preservation and power, and some of them in fact aid us in our striving; some passions are useful, and some are not. Spinoza defines "good" as "what we certainly know to be useful to us", and "evil" as "what we certainly know prevents us from being masters of some good". Thus the distinction between good and evil, for Spinoza, amounts to a distinction between what is good *for us* and what is bad *for us*. With this understanding of the terms, Spinoza can establish a kind of morality. The morality is egoistic, meaning that it is grounded ultimately in self-interest. Still, Spinoza thinks that rational egoism will lead us into a lifestyle that is ethical in a familiar way – a lifestyle in which we are genuinely concerned for others.

> **KEY POINTS**
> - Humans often struggle against forces in the environment. To the extent that humans are self-governed, or are able to use outside things to further their ends, they are (in a sense) *free*.
> - A perfectly free human being would actively pursue his or her own power and knowledge, without any concern for others, except in so far as others bring some benefit to the free human being.
> - Perfect freedom is impossible for us because of the various ways that we are subject to passions and forces beyond our control. Still, we can work towards greater freedom, even if total freedom is impossible. To the extent that we succeed, we will be *virtuous* (in Spinoza's sense).

Spinoza's ethics

How can Spinoza turn rational self-interest into any kind of genuine concern for the welfare of other human beings? The key is the recognition that individual human beings can gain great benefits by forming a community with their fellow human beings. And a community will work only if its members show real awareness of one another's needs, rights and privileges. So we compromise. If we were left to our own devices, we could ignore our neighbours, or disdain them, or even do harm to them, as we liked. Nothing in Spinoza's philosophy makes these attitudes especially wrong – just counterproductive. If we really want to enhance our chances for survival and flourishing, we shall rein in those inclinations and instead find a way to live harmoniously with our neighbours, so that we may obtain all the benefits of a society – such as police protection, division of labour, sewer systems and so on. We agree to abide by rules (and so voluntarily limit our natural powers of action) for the sake of belonging to communities that will be more useful to us in the long run. Thus it *pays* to concern ourselves with others.

In uniting ourselves with others, we become part of a stronger being. As Spinoza writes:

> To man, I say, there is nothing more useful than man. Man, I say, can wish for nothing more helpful to the preservation of his being than that all should so agree in all things that the Minds and Bodies of all would compose, as it were, one Mind and one Body; that all should strive together, as far as they can,

> to preserve their being; and that all, together, should seek for
> themselves the common advantage of all. (E 4p18s)

The last claim of this passage is that humans should take as their own goal the advantage of the community to which they belong. In other words, we should take the interest of society as our own interest. We shall want our society to flourish and grow in strength, for our own sakes; we shall seek its health as we would seek our own. In deciding what to do or not to do in our community, we should be asking ourselves, "Am I contributing to the overall health of this greater body?" For if I am not, I am hurting the very thing that I am hoping will enhance my own life.

Of course, we all know cases where we can commit a small crime against others or against society that will help us individually without causing *significant* harm to our community. Take littering, for instance; it is much easier to toss a can onto the ground than to find a proper receptacle, and it is hard to be persuaded that we are doing significant harm to society by this action. Or consider cheating a little on our taxes: that clearly benefits us individually, and it will not bring society crashing down around us. Typically, when we think about such examples, we are tempted to ask something along the lines of "What if everybody did that?" Spinoza makes a similar type of reply in the course of arguing that a truly free man would never act deceptively. He argues that the best life is the one that is based on rational self-interest; but in so far as we make rational judgements, we are making judgements that we would recommend *all* humans to make, in so far as they are rational; and since we cannot want *all* humans to litter or cheat on their taxes (or act deceptively), we cannot rationally want it for ourselves.

But this kind of argument (which is very similar to the kind of argument Kant advances in his moral theory) does not fit very well with the self-interested egoism Spinoza places at the base of his own theory. Recall that Spinoza thinks we are essentially selfish, amoral snobs who do whatever it takes to survive and grow in strength. If we have to check our little schemes against the question "Can I will all human beings to do the same?", then our plans of action will be severely restricted; indeed, all the "egoism" of the theory seems to evaporate. Is Spinoza just trying to sneak in some traditional morality through the back door?

The guidance of reason

This raises a deep question about the nature of Spinoza's moral theory. At first it seems as if Spinoza's theory is based on a familiar and straightforward rational egoism: we behave "morally" (in the traditional sense of the term) because, on the whole, it pays off. "Rationality" here means strategic, self-interested action. But then, when we consider situations in which being "moral" does not pay off, Spinoza suggests that there is still some vestige of rationality within us that will keep us from cheating. In this second type of situation, though, "rationality" refers to something more abstract, as if there is a core of pure reason in each human being which dictates that we all should follow the same universal laws. The first kind of rationality is self-interested, while the second is disinterested. Which one does Spinoza think best characterizes human nature?

It may be that Spinoza thinks it is the first one, and then (for some of us, anyway) also the other. Recall that Spinoza thinks we are often ignorant about many things – what nature is, how it works, what is truly good for us, what will bring us joy. We are also often ignorant about ourselves and what we truly desire. Perhaps the early parts of our lives include basic wants, for food and play and security and warmth. Then we graduate to more adult desires – for status, luxury, money, friendships and love. Many of us, when asked what we really want, might list many or all of these things; we think that these are our deepest desires. And Spinoza thinks that, typically, we act in rationally self-interested ways to obtain these things. Indeed, this kind of rational self-interest, combined with these desires, is enough to motivate us to join a community and act in "moral" ways at least most of the time. It is enough to make us, on the whole, fairly responsible members of our community.

But a few of us graduate to a deeper knowledge of ourselves. We find that our desires for status, luxury and so on are not really our deepest desires; we discover that they will not bring us any lasting joy. So we seek out our deeper desires and try to satisfy them. This is precisely how Spinoza describes his own situation at the beginning of his *Treatise on the Emendation of the Intellect*:

> After experience had taught me that all the things which regularly occur in ordinary life are empty and futile, and I saw that all the things which were the cause or object of my fear had nothing of good or bad in themselves, except insofar as my

> mind was moved by them, I resolved at last to try to find out whether there was anything which would be the true good, capable of communicating itself, and which alone would affect the mind, all others being rejected – whether there was something which, once found and acquired, would continuously give me the greatest joy, to eternity. (TEI: §1)

In this *Treatise*, Spinoza tries to discover what will satisfy the deepest striving of his own mind. What he discovers is that his mind, above all else, seeks the joy that comes from an understanding of the most profound things. He begins to see himself as motivated by the desire for understanding, rather than for the desires for fame and riches and ordinary pleasures.

It is clear that Spinoza thinks that he is not just speaking for himself. He thinks that all of us are motivated by this deep desire – although certainly not all of us know it. Most of us do not stop to realize that the things we are pursuing are not giving us any lasting happiness; we just keep chasing faster and faster, in the hope that we will be finally satisfied. In this case we are like a thirsty person gulping down seawater, which only makes us thirstier.

So the wise human, Spinoza thinks, will try to live a life under what he calls the "guidance of reason". In this case, reason is not just thinking strategically about how to get what we want; it *tells* us what to want:

> Since reason demands nothing contrary to nature, it demands that everyone love himself, seek his own advantage, what is really useful to him, want what will really lead man to a greater perfection, and, absolutely, that everyone should strive to preserve his own being as far as he can. This, indeed, is as necessarily true as that the whole is greater than its parts.
> (E 4p18s)

Spinoza goes on to demonstrate that reason will demand that we perfect our strengths – in particular, our knowledge and understanding. And we shall find that our highest goal will be to understand the ultimate thing in existence, that is, God. In so far as we live under the guidance of reason, we shall all set aside our pursuit of shallow joys and strive for our greater perfection, which is the knowledge of God. And if we know that we have done this as well as we possibly can, Spinoza thinks we will enjoy a state of "self-esteem", which he says is the highest thing we can hope for.

Now such a wise human being might have more reason than the rest of us for behaving in a recognizably "moral" way. Spinoza argues that the wise person will recognize that in so far as humans live under the guidance of reason, there will be more agreement among them and less strife and controversy, for the same reason he will tell them all to do the same thing. So, the thought goes, wise humans should want to live the life they would endorse for all wise humans; they will want to follow the rules they want everyone to follow, in so far as they are rational. They will want this because they know that, deep down, we are all striving towards becoming the perfectly rational human being – in other words, our old friend, the free man. The free man, according to Spinoza, "hates no one, is angry with no one, envies no one, is indignant with no one, scorns no one, and is not at all proud" (E 4p73s); he furthermore knows that "hate is to be conquered by returning love, and that everyone who is led by reason desires for others also the good he wants for himself" (*ibid.*). He is a secular saint, so to speak, since his moral way of life is rooted in an adequate understanding of nature and his own psychology, and he lives his life under the strict guidance of reason.

The sage and society

We have, then, a two-level account of Spinoza's ethics. On the lower level, most of us are motivated to follow society's rules because of what society gives us in return: civic order, leisure time, communal resources, protection and so on. It is a good deal – nothing more, nothing less. On the upper level, a few of us – those blessed with greater wisdom – understand that our own rational nature demands that we live our lives under the guidance of reason, and this reason demands a life that is "good" in both the traditional sense and in Spinoza's sense. We live healthy, constructive, joyous lives, for the sake of being healthy, constructive and joyous human beings. Virtue, for the sage, is its own reward.

The problem is that the two levels have to exist together, since society is made up of all sorts of people. So how can society guarantee that the "low levels" will continue to obey the rules even when breaking them will bring them some small benefit? And how will the "high levels" behave when, in an imperfect society, the guidance of reason will bring about certain harm or death?

Let us take the second question first. In a society of sages, following the guidance of reason would be easy, presumably. Such a society might not even need laws, since everyone would be following the dictates of a univocal reason. But when those sages are placed in an imperfect society – one that is perhaps governed by "low levels" – then following reason may not be the smartest course of action. Imagine, for example, a society that requires its members to be Christians, on pain of death. The sage is called before the court and asked, "Are you a Christian?" The sage, remembering Spinoza's *Ethics*, realizes that "A free man always acts honestly, not deceptively." What is the sage to do? Telling the truth – the truth about Spinoza's conception of God or Nature – means certain death, which obviously is "evil", according to Spinoza. So it seems that the sage must compromise, and act deceptively on this occasion, perhaps with the hope of later working towards reforming society in a more rational direction. The "higher levels" in general, it seems, need to accommodate themselves to the society around them, and live as rationally as circumstances permit.

What about getting the "low levels" to obey the law? There are two ways of bringing this about. First, the society can threaten them with severe punishments if they are ever caught breaking the laws. Fear is a powerful force, and fear of severe punishments might induce many "low levels" to obey the law even when it seems implausible that they will get caught breaking it. "Certainly," a "low level" might think, "I could probably get away with stealing the bread, but if somehow I were caught, my hand would be cut off, and the benefits just are not worth the risk." We can count on the power of the passions to keep "low levels" in line, thus turning a philosophical weakness into a civic virtue.

The second way of keeping the "low levels" in line also makes use of the passions. Spinoza recognizes that religion can exert a powerful influence over human behaviour, and in fact he thinks the chief aim of any religion is to get people to behave in a moral fashion. Believing in an all-powerful God, who watches over us at every instant, and will reward virtuous behaviour and punish disobedience, gives someone a very strong incentive to be moral. God is a perfect policeman and judge, filling in wherever the human police and judges fail. Spinoza thinks it is wise to get the "low levels" to believe this, even if the "high levels" will understand (after reading the *Ethics*) that it is the wrong way to think about God.

> **KEY POINTS**
> - It is rational for us to seek the comforts and protection of a civil society, and to treat others well in so far as this is required of us in order to belong to such a society.
> - Our moral concern for others is initially self-interested; as we become more rational, we feel further obligation to live the life determined through pure reason (that is, to live the life of a free man, so far as we are able).
> - A thoroughly rational person can be expected to be a good citizen; those who do not live under the guidance of reason must be persuaded to be good citizens by the threat of punishment and the influence of illusory religious ideas.

Spinoza's politics

We have already seen Spinoza's account of why a political state should come about. In a state of nature, where each individual fends for herself, life will be extremely difficult. It would be even difficult to sleep at night, since we would worry that someone might come along and kill us and steal our belongings. But by cooperating with others we can make life easier and have a much better chance of satisfying our *conatus* for self-preservation. So we form a "social contract" and we all agree to follow a certain set of rules, or follow the orders of some leader who can organize our efforts.

Now the social contract will work only so long as there is some means for enforcing it, since, as we have seen, there may be many opportunities for us to break the rules and take advantage of our fellow citizens' good will. So, in establishing a political state, we have to give our leader – the *sovereign* – the power to enforce the rules. This will mean a loss of power on our part; we allow the sovereign to enforce rules that will often prove costly for us (for example, we may authorize the sovereign to punish speeders, and then be caught ourselves). Still, on the whole, we are better off than we would be in a state of nature; and this is what legitimates political authority, according to Spinoza.

In moving from a state of nature to a political state, we have to decide what kind of sovereign we want. The easiest route is *monarchy*: we decide that one person should rule us all, through the service of an army or police force. We can even entrust that one person to select his or her successor. The problem, of course, is that the one person may be particularly unsuitable for the job. The monarch may exact heavy taxes, or place harsh burdens upon the citizens – so harsh that the citizens may be prompted to revolt, since it becomes less clear that the state of nature is more dangerous than life under a tyrannical thug. Next, we might consider a kind of *aristocracy*, or some form of government in which the citizens are ruled by a small group of privileged persons. But the same problems may emerge – the aristocracy may decide to exploit the citizens to such an extent that revolution becomes an attractive idea. In the end, Spinoza thinks the most stable form of government will be some kind of *representative democracy*, since such a government will naturally limit the ways in which the citizens are exploited. Furthermore, the danger of revolution becomes remote, since the citizens would essentially be revolting against themselves.

In his *Theological-Political Treatise*, Spinoza presents this argument by retracing the history of the Jews, who are lead first by Moses, and then by tribal leaders or priests. Moses, Spinoza thinks, was an effective and capable leader, whom the Jews largely obeyed, but Moses did not appoint a single successor. That is a danger inherent in monarchy: many battles have been waged over succession to the throne. The Jews were then led by several leaders, with the result that the tribes became separate political states, and so the original unified state was dissolved. But at various points in the history of the Jews the people ruled themselves, and during these times there was very little civic unrest. Though Spinoza thinks it would be unwise to model a modern political state on the example of the ancient Jews, he does think some general lessons may be learned: particularly, the lesson that concentrating political power in the hands of one person or a few people typically leads to political instability. If we want to join ourselves to a larger, long-lasting, stable body, then we are well advised to join a representative democracy.

Spinoza wrote the *Theological-Political Treatise* (as well as a separate *Political Treatise*, which was unfinished at the time of his death) not just to make a general point about politics, but also to address the specific circumstances of the Netherlands at the time. The Netherlands had been ruled by William II, who died in 1650. His son was too young to assume the throne, so the various provinces of the Netherlands were united into a kind of congress, called the States-General, under the leadership of Jan De Witt. As William III became an adult towards the later 1660s, he and his supporters sought to re-establish the monarchy. Spinoza opposed this idea, and wrote the *Theological-Political Treatise* in 1670 in part to help advance the cause of Dutch democracy. But times were difficult. The Dutch Republic was at war with England,

and many people thought they needed a monarch in a time of war. William III took over in 1672, and an angry mob murdered De Witt and his brother. Spinoza, it is said, had to be physically restrained from protesting the mob's action.

Spinoza's critique of theology

Spinoza's reasons for writing the *Theological-Political Treatise* were not merely political, of course; they were also theological. It is clear that, from Spinoza's perspective, traditional religion – whether in his day or ours – is radically wrong. Spinoza thinks that God is an impersonal substance, acting necessarily from its own nature, bringing about our world and the events in it as inevitably as theorems roll out from axioms in geometry. It would be misguided to try to pray to such a thing, or to expect that events will be arranged for our own peculiar benefit. Yet traditional religions conceive of God as very humanlike – they *anthropomorphize* God, as Spinoza would say – with definite goals, desires and passions. Believers think they can affect what God does by putting in requests, and when God does not comply, they think it is because God has some better end in store for us. Moreover, they use God as an explanation whenever they come across natural events they cannot explain.

At the same time, Spinoza thinks there is a political use for all these wrong-headed beliefs about God. Believing that God is a great, invisible policeman enforcing obedience to moral commandments helps to keep the peace in civil society. So his *Theological-Political Treatise* tries to maintain a delicate balance. He nowhere says outright that all these traditional beliefs are nonsense. In fact, he says explicitly that the Bible is an excellent guide for living a moral life, and he thinks a state would do well to require its citizens to embody the fundamental virtues that the Bible recommends. At the same time, though, he wants to question many of the metaphysical claims theologians make on the basis of the Bible – claims about what God is and whether God sometimes interferes with the laws of nature – and he wants to argue that people should be allowed to philosophize freely and without religious censorship. So Spinoza wants to "de-fang" religion, supporting its power to motivate moral behaviour while shutting down its authority to tell us what to say and think about the world. In the end, Spinoza has to say that the authors of scripture knew a lot about how to be moral, but really did not know anything about science, metaphysics or philosophy.

And this is exactly what he does say. From his studies early on in the Jewish school in Amsterdam, Spinoza had thorough knowledge of the Bible and Hebrew. In chapter after chapter, he carefully examines the Bible and makes acute observations about ambiguities in the text, about the different writing styles and about what we can deduce regarding authorship, about the psychological temperaments of various prophets, and about the historical and cultural circumstances of the ancient Jews. Indeed, some scholars have identified the *Theological-Political Treatise* as the first work in modern biblical study, since Spinoza was among the first to treat the Bible in the same scholarly way that we would normally treat any ancient text. What Spinoza concludes is that the authors of the Bible were pre-scientific, and wrote at a time when events were often exaggerated and expressed in metaphorical and mythological ways. For example, an important event, in which a smaller army defeated a larger one, might be described as a legion of enemies falling under the swords of only a handful of righteous men, with angels battling at their side. Pessimistic prophets saw God as angry, with terrible wrath and fury; gentle-minded prophets imagined God as loving and merciful. God was often described in terms that would make the greatest impression upon the people of the time (sitting on a fiery throne, perhaps), and not with anything approaching metaphysical exactitude. Thus the Bible tells us much more about the psychologies of ancient authors and their readers than it does about God.

But, throughout all of the Bible, there is a moral teaching that Spinoza regards as highly valuable. He identifies seven "Dogmas of the Universal Faith", which he thinks are the Bible's central teachings. The dogmas are as follows:

1. God is a supreme being and is both just and merciful.
2. God is one alone.
3. Nothing can be concealed from God.
4. Everyone is required to obey God.
5. Obeying God means being just and showing love to one's neighbour.
6. All and only those who obey God are saved.
7. God forgives sinners who repent.

These dogmas are what the Bible is really about, according to Spinoza; it does not intend to produce a plausible metaphysics or cosmology. Its aim is to get people to believe these dogmas – or at least behave *as if* they believe them. The authors of scripture were geniuses at grasping what people ought to believe in order to promote civic harmony. And so the aim of theology generally, Spinoza thinks, is not philosophical truth but rather *obedience*.

The freedom to philosophize

Of course, Spinoza himself did not believe all the Dogmas of the Universal Faith. He did not think God was any kind of judge who could show justice, mercy or forgiveness, and he did not believe people are "saved" in the sense of being admitted to heaven. Still, he saw that the dogmas are just what we should want the "low levels" (described earlier) to believe. The "high levels" do not need to believe them, since they have strong philosophical reasons for being just and showing love to one's neighbour. So, with the twin efforts of both theology and philosophy, all people can be motivated to live moral lives.

It is because he saw theology's focus as *obedience* and philosophy's target as *truth* that Spinoza thought philosophers should be accorded the freedom to think as they like and say what they think. So he argued that political authorities should not censor the writings of philosophers: after all, the "low levels" will not have any interest in philosophical arguments, and will be motivated towards moral behaviour through religion, and the "high levels" will already understand that being moral is in their best interest. But we can all see what is wrong with this argument. The political authorities in Spinoza's day believed that certain philosophical writings can undermine all people's confidence in religious dogmas – whether "high" or "low" – and they also believed that if a person did not believe in an omniscient and omnipotent being who polices our behaviour, then that person would be an *atheist*, and have no real motivation to be moral. Spinoza himself was later branded as an atheist (despite the fact that he did not believe in anything *but* God!), since the "God" described in the *Ethics* was not the right kind of policing god. The thought was that if many people read the *Ethics* – or heard enough about it – then they might well lose the incentive to be upright Christians and, as a consequence, embark upon sinful and criminal lives.

Spinoza might reply that anyone inclined to read the *Ethics* (or other philosophical works) would already be capable of appreciating the motivations to be moral that arise out of purely rational self-interest. In other words, anyone intelligent enough to be thinking philosophically already sees the reasons for being moral; and everyone else is covered by religion. There may be something to this. If it really is in our own best interest to be good members of society, then we should expect that anyone who (for philosophical or anti-religious reasons) decides to rebel against society would quickly learn the error of their ways and reconsider their assumptions. Over the long run, we might say, the truth will out, and anti-societal rebellion will be extinguished. But it is hard to be confident of this argument, since groups of humans continually act irrationally and chase after absurd and self-destructive ends – a point Spinoza would readily concede.

KEY POINTS

- Spinoza believes that the most stable form of government is a democratic republic, since people will be less likely to revolt against a government in which they take part.
- The state ought to encourage a broad, basic religion, since it will help to encourage less rational people to behave morally.
- The state should allow philosophers the freedom to say what they want, since philosophers are supposed to be rational enough not to say anything to the general populace that will upset civic harmony.

Spinoza's psychotherapy

As important as they are, let us retreat from these broader political concerns. Spinoza thought deeply about them, but at the same time he also constructed for himself a safe refuge in which he could keep himself insulated from all the ups and downs of political change, and indeed, all the ups and downs of human life. The last part of the *Ethics* begins by advancing twenty or so propositions that describe ways in which certain passions can be strengthened or weakened. From these propositions we can construct a Spinozistic psychotherapy – a five-step programme we should follow if we want to reduce our slavery to harmful passions.

For example, suppose that you are suffering from depression. No course of action seems attractive, other than sitting motionless for hours on end. Even food and drink are not appealing. Tears come for no reason at all. Here are the steps Spinoza thinks you should take, if you can, to overcome this dreadful condition:

1. *Understand the affect.* You first need to understand what is happening to you psychologically and physiologically. Your understanding must be as clear and distinct as possible: a *clinical* understanding, so to speak.
2. *Separate cause from effect.* You then need to understand what in fact is causing this condition. Perhaps, in this instance, your life's inherent worthlessness is not causing your depression; perhaps the depression is being caused by something less dramatic, such as your diet, or some flaw in your body's production of biochemicals, or the loss of a job or a pet and so on.
3. *Meditate upon this.* Next, you need to remind yourself, as you experience the symptoms of depression, what is really going on; you must get used to associating the true cause of your feelings with the feelings themselves. Over time, the clear understanding will replace the foggy one. And typically, when we know what is causing an uneasy feeling, we are better able to cope with that feeling.
4. *Relate your understanding to fixed features of the universe.* This may sound grandiose, but in cases where the depression cannot be straightforwardly cured through diet or medication, your best bet (Spinoza thinks) is to understand how what you are experiencing is a perfectly natural result of the way the universe is. A scientist coming to understand the phenomenon of depression does not necessarily become depressed; instead, she comes to appreciate the intricate networks of causes and conditions that bring the depression about (and perhaps she is even excited about it). You should adopt the same attitude: be as intellectually fascinated with your own condition (and detached from it) as an independent observer would be.
5. *Train yourself to maintain this understanding.* Finally, you need to take steps to preserve the understanding you have gained, and protect yourself from sliding back into your previous state. Perhaps you will impose upon yourself some rule, such as, "Whenever I begin staring off into space, I must immediately get up and read the scholium to proposition 10 of Spinoza's *Ethics*, part 5." Or perhaps you will identify places that you associate with your depression (such as the corner tavern) and stop going there. Develop some rules or tricks that will help you to maintain your clinical and detached understanding of your condition.

Now Spinoza would be the first to admit that this self-help programme will not always work. Some affects just run too deep, and no effort of our understanding will displace them. Moreover, we are all doomed to fail in the end, remember; we will lose the battle against our environment and grow weak and die. But *sometimes* we are able to rule over our affects, instead of being ruled by them, and Spinoza thinks that this psychotherapy is a sound strategy for gaining an advantage over our passions.

The eternity of the mind

Following this psychotherapy comes one of the most puzzling sections of the *Ethics*, and of Spinoza's philosophy as a whole. The last propositions of the *Ethics* concern Spinoza's doctrine of the eternity of the mind: the way in which the mind never dies.

There are two general puzzles about this block of propositions. First, Spinoza's doctrine of parallelism holds that the mind and the body are the same thing, conceived under two different attributes. But we know the body will eventually die and disintegrate. Hence the first puzzle: how can anything of the mind survive? The second puzzle has to do with the different ways in which Spinoza writes of "eternity". In several places he points out that "eternity" does not mean an endless time, but instead *timelessness*. But in other places he seems to imply that, as we gain adequate understanding of things, a larger portion of our mind is eternal. The puzzle is how more and more of a thing can *become* timeless. Shall we say that, *in the past*, only a third was timeless, but *now* over half is timeless?

It is safe to say that no one has made complete sense of this part of Spinoza's philosophy. But we can perhaps piece together a view that Spinoza could develop that captures most (though not all) of what Spinoza says. The view consists of three observations.

First, let us recall that, according to Spinoza's philosophy, there is an infinite mind in nature, just as there is an infinite body (the physical universe). In this infinite mind (or the "infinite intellect", as Spinoza calls it) are the ideas of all existent things. We might think of this infinite intellect as a Great Big Book of Everything, containing perfectly precise, accurate and adequate accounts of absolutely everything that happens in the universe: "At time t1, *x* happens; at time t2, *y* happens; at time t3, ..." This book could be called "eternal" in the sense that its existence has nothing to do with time: it is never more true at one time than another, and it does not change.

Next, we should recognize that whenever we gain an adequate understanding of anything, we have in our minds the same idea that is present in the infinite intellect. The account in our mind, in other words, is the same as the account present in the Great Big Book of Everything. In that sense, when we understand something adequately, part of our mind *becomes* eternal; of course, the account is in the Book eternally, but the account has only now become part of our mind. Furthermore, since there are common notions that have always been essential to our minds, and common notions are perfectly adequate, there has always been something pertaining to the essence of our minds that is eternal.

Finally, we have also seen that the greatest striving of the mind is to gain adequate knowledge. To the extent that we do, we experience joy, since the mind grows in strength and perfection. When we come to know things through the third kind of knowledge, we experience the greatest possible intellectual joy. In these circumstances, we associate this great joy with the idea of God, since the third kind of knowledge consists in seeing immediately how things are related to God's essence. Thus we experience *the intellectual love of God* – something that seems to make Spinoza nearly giddy with enthusiasm.

As I warned, this view does not make sense of everything Spinoza says about the eternity of the mind, but it does capture the main points, and is broadly consistent with the rest of his metaphysics. Several scholars have suspected that Spinoza was carried away by his passions in writing this part of the *Ethics* – in the end, he wanted to have some kind of afterlife, and he felt he could get away with this much. Other scholars have thought that Spinoza's apparent enthusiasm is only a subterfuge that allows the superficial reader to think that Spinoza offers an afterlife, when a more careful reader will see through the ruse. (But by this late point in the *Ethics*, why would Spinoza suddenly wish to play it safe?)

Setting this controversy aside, we can still ask what kind of afterlife one gets from this doctrine of the eternity of the mind. The answer depends on how we understand Spinoza's temperament. If we think of Spinoza as a strict rationalist, then the answer is: not much. Consider the fact that every adequate idea you will ever have is already eternally present in the infinite intellect; if you want to know what your experience after death will be, the answer is that it will be just the same as it was before your birth. There is no more reason to get excited over this kind of afterlife than there would be if we were assured that, even after death, our names would continue to be published in the phone book.

On the other hand, if we think of Spinoza not as a rationalist, but as a mystic (as some scholars do), then perhaps there is a kind of extraordinary experience we enjoy in virtue of being parts of the infinite intellect. In ordinary temporal experience, we do not experience timelessness. But rare moments come along – perhaps moments Spinoza would describe as the intellectual love of God – in which we feel lost in metaphysical contemplation, and perhaps part of some eternal mind. As Spinoza writes,

> Though it is impossible that we should recollect that we existed before the body – since there cannot be traces of this in the body, and eternity can neither be defined by time nor have any relation to time – still, we feel and know by experience that we are eternal. For the mind feels those things that it conceives in understanding no less than those it has in memory.
>
> (E 5p23s)

Perhaps Spinoza himself, as he crafted the deductive structure of the *Ethics*, at times felt that he was rising above time and joining in some eternal realm of ideas; honest mathematicians will report this kind of thrill. And perhaps Spinoza sought for some way to include this extraordinary experience in his philosophy, even if it did not fit very neatly with other things he had demonstrated in a cooler state of mind.

Key points

- Spinoza believes that rational self-interest provides the beginning of a foundation for a stable civic society. To that foundation must be added either religious beliefs (to encourage morality) or the guidance of reason (for those capable of it).
- The ideal human being is one who lives under the guidance of reason. This person is fully autonomous, and follows the dictates of reason which rule impartially over all. To the extent we achieve this, we are virtuous.
- The most stable state is a democratic republic. Such a republic should allow free speech.
- We can attain some mastery over our passions through understanding them and keeping in mind the necessity of all things.
- Our greatest joy is the intellectual love of God, which comes from an intuitive or rational knowledge of the way in which all things are in God. This also gives our minds a kind of eternity.

five

Leibniz's world of monads

Leibniz's life

Gottfried Wilhelm Leibniz was born in 1646 into a troubled and imperfect world. The Thirty Years' War, raging since 1618, had cut Germany's population in half. Leibniz's father was a professor of philosophy at the University of Leipzig, and although he barely came to know his son (he died when Leibniz was only 6), he had just enough time to recognize and take pride in Leibniz's precocious intelligence. Leibniz and his sister were raised by their loving mother, and Leibniz devoted much of his childhood to reading his way through his father's library, mastering Latin and Greek along the way. He enrolled in the University of Leipzig when he was 15. Only two years later he produced a thesis in metaphysics; three years after that he published a short work in mathematics; and soon thereafter he was awarded a doctoral degree in jurisprudence. It would be in these three fields – metaphysics, mathematics and justice – that Leibniz would invest his intellectual efforts for the rest of his life. The world described by his philosophy would have at its core a profound metaphysics, an elegant mathematical harmony, and an uncompromised guarantee of divine justice. In short, the world he envisioned had everything war-ravaged Germany lacked.

At the age of 20, Leibniz was offered a professorship at the University of Altdorf, but he declined, deciding instead to try to make a greater contribution to the unstable political world around him. His plan, no doubt, was to develop his philosophical vision in greater depth and detail, and then to share his wisdom with the rulers of the world so that together they could forge a just and more rational government. Thus began his lifelong career of service to various royal persons – dukes and counts, mostly, including a few who became kings and queens. But the royal figures he served typically expected more mundane services from him (such as tracing royal genealogies), and they often grew impatient when Leibniz spent his time instead on much grander projects. They showed little interest in his utopian political plans, and no interest at all in his brilliant visions in mathematics and metaphysics. So much of Leibniz's life was spent chasing one royal patron after another, hoping to find one who would fully recognize, reward and support his mission. He never found one. His life is the sad story of a brilliant man ready to turn all of his intellectual energies towards making the world a better place, and who experienced mainly rejection and neglect. By the time of his death in 1716 he was a nearly forgotten man, and his grave went unmarked for 50 years.

Leibniz wrote two philosophical books in his lifetime (one published posthumously), along with scores of brief essays and articles. Prominent philosophers such as Christian Wolff and Immanuel Kant recognized his importance and helped to make other philosophers aware of his philosophy, but a systematic and comprehensive catalogue of Leibniz's unpublished works was not available until the end of the nineteenth century. Only then was it discovered that he had written about 15,000 letters and 40,000 other works, ranging from short essays to lengthy tracts. A project to publish a critical edition of his works began in 1901. The project continues to this day, and now there are about fifty volumes published in this series, with many more to come. In addition to developing a profound metaphysics and philosophical theology (which we shall examine in this chapter and in Chapter 6), Leibniz is also credited with independently discovering calculus at the same time Isaac Newton did. He also wrote extensively about the political world of his day, including lengthy works regarding European relations with Egypt and China, and he proposed several innovations in mining technology. There is hardly a single topic he did not address in some work or other. As we shall see, Leibniz claimed in his metaphysics that each mind reflects the entire universe; but the breadth of his interests suggests that perhaps he was only generalizing from his own case.

It is difficult to say much about Leibniz's personal life. He seems not to have had one. His mother died when he was 18, and his sister died two years later. He never married, and we have no evidence that he was ever romantically involved with anyone. (As one biographer notes, not one of his 15,000 letters could count as a love letter.) A story is told that Leibniz once proposed marriage to a woman when he was 50 years old. But she requested time to think it over, and by the time she decided, Leibniz had moved on to other projects. It is clear, though, that he had many social charms and was able to make friends easily. He travelled extensively throughout Europe and relished the lively culture of Paris. He maintained correspondences with scores of interesting people. He also developed philosophical friendships with various royal women, including Descartes's friend Elisabeth; her sister, the Electress Sophia of Hanover; and Sophia's daughter, Sophia Charlotte, the first queen of Prussia. He was a great conciliator, seeking to find the ways in which all previous philosophers and theologians had each gained an accurate perspective on the truth – that is, the ways in which every great philosopher had anticipated (though perhaps in a confused way) Leibniz's own grand metaphysical system.

Philosophical spirit

In overall philosophical spirit, Leibniz was very similar to Thomas Aquinas, who constructed an ingenious synthesis of Aristotle's natural philosophy with the fundamental tenets of Christianity. There is a definite sense in which Leibniz wanted to be the new seventeenth-century Aquinas, synthesizing the new mechanical physics of Galileo, Descartes and Huygens (and Leibniz) with both Protestant and Catholic forms of Christianity. At the same time, he also sought to preserve the deep philosophical insights of both Plato and Aristotle, and show what truth there is in both rationalism and empiricism. In brief, he wanted to unearth the truth in every great philosophy and forge a metaphysical system to which all thinkers (from all ages) could subscribe. He was a consummate synthesizer. In reviewing Leibniz's metaphysics, it is important to keep this in mind, since at times he may appear to be concerned with doctrines few of us now take interest in. They are of interest to Leibniz precisely because someone he respected took them to be true, and Leibniz wanted to see the truth in them for himself.

So we shall find in Leibniz's system a very strange combination of philosophical bedfellows, so to speak. We shall find that the laws of collision determine every effect; but also that bodies do not really exert causal influence over one another. We shall find that every truth is analytic, that is, true in virtue of the meanings of the terms; but also that some truths are still contingent (that is, they could have been otherwise). We shall find that each substance mirrors the rest of the universe from its own point of view; but also that, strictly speaking, substances cannot perceive anything outside themselves. Leibniz's philosophy was packed to maximal capacity: he fitted as many philosophical views into it as anyone possibly could, and adding even just one more would cause the thing to burst.

We must also take note of one philosopher who provided a strong *negative* influence on Leibniz: Spinoza, whom Leibniz visited in the Hague in 1670. As recounted in previous chapters, Spinoza believed in an impersonal divine being whose nature necessitated all things in the strongest possible sense. At one point in his life, Leibniz was inclined to this view; as a rationalist, he found the force of Spinoza's logic attractive and compelling. But (as he later recounted) Leibniz pulled himself back from "this dangerous precipice" by taking seriously the great number of things that are merely possible and never actual. Certainly, it seems, there *could* have been dogs with antlers, or warm-blooded frogs, or patrons with great stashes of money dedicated towards funding Leibniz's pursuits, despite the fact that in the actual world there turns out to have been none. Once we admit these possibilities as genuine, Spinoza's necessitarianism melts away, and we must search for some explanation for why what is actual is actual, and why what is merely possible does not exist. This concern – to preserve genuine contingency and thus avoid Spinoza's dreaded doctrine of necessity – exerted a powerful pull over Leibniz's philosophical trajectory. Very often Leibniz rejected a view simply because he saw that it would lead to Spinozism, and that, he believed, was enough to show that the view was false. As one commentator has said, Leibniz was influenced by many philosophers, but he was *haunted* by Spinoza.

The basic metaphysical picture

It is difficult to provide a comprehensive picture of Leibniz's metaphysics, and not only because it is packed to maximal capacity. It is difficult also because Leibniz took many years in developing his "mature metaphysics", and many commentators are still busy sorting out the various positions Leibniz worked out on the way to his final resting place. But we shall try to begin with a sketch of his mature worldview, and then turn in subsequent sections to more detailed treatments of its particular features.

To get an initial grip on Leibniz's metaphysics, we shall employ an imaginative device. Try to imagine, if you will, the entire collection of all spatial points in the universe – every point throughout the whole of space, from a point at the end of your little finger to a point on the highest mountain on Mars; from a point in the middle of the Atlantic to the point at the centre of the sun, and so on. It is an incredibly vast collection of points, as infinite as the reach of space itself, and infinite on the small scale as well, since any region or object we care to describe will itself contain infinitely many points inside its borders. But we will not let this stop us; let us begin with all of them. Now imagine furthermore that each one of these points is something like a recording station: each point records everything that has happened, is happening and will happen, in the whole universe, from its own point of view. Each point has its camera always running, so to speak, pointed in all directions and aiming at all distances. Of course, the points will have clearer and more accurate information about some events, and they will be somewhat murkier about others. But each point reflects and records everything, with varying degrees of clarity, from its own perspective.

So far, so good. We need to make two further moves to arrive at Leibniz's basic metaphysical view. First, suppose now that these points do not *really* perceive or observe what is going throughout the universe. Instead, suppose all the information about what is going on elsewhere is *internal* to them. Each point comes "pre-programmed" with all its perceptions in it. Strictly speaking, no information or signal passes from one point to another, though it might seem as if signals are sent, since when there is a change at one point, that change shows up in all the other points. But this is an instance of marvellous coordination and synchronization, not an instance of passing signals. Each point is a world unto itself, with nothing passing into it or out of it. But the perceptions stored up within these points are so marvellously synchronized that it is just as if information were passing smoothly among them. The points are, let us say, harmonized perfectly with one another. Leibniz calls this "*universal harmony*".

That is the first step. The second step – and this is a big step – is to eliminate the space that supposedly houses these points. The points are sizeless, and have no location in any space whatsoever.

This last step may seem to pull the rug out from under us. For we started with space in order to imagine all the points contained within space, and to make sense of what these points would perceive and how they would all be harmonized with one another. But once we have all the perceptions packed into each point, and we have cut off all interactions among the points, there is no longer any need for space. It adds no further information to the story. It was just a device to get our metaphysics off the ground, and we can now discard it.

The resulting picture gives us a broadly accurate view of Leibniz's metaphysics. The "points" we have been talking about are called *monads* by Leibniz. Each monad is a substance, containing within itself all its past, present and future states. It also contains stores of information about all the other monads. Monads do not genuinely interact with one another, and they are not located in space. Each of them is like a Cartesian soul – immaterial, non-extended, and able to represent things. There is a vast infinity of monads, just as we typically think of there being a vast infinity of points in space. The more familiar world of bodies, rocks, animals and stars (and points in space) somehow arises out of the information stored in the monads: the monads are fundamentally real, and the familiar world *supervenes upon* them (or "rides upon" them).

The world of bodies

With this in mind, it may help us to think of Leibniz's metaphysics as occupying two levels. At the basic level there is an infinite collection of mind-like monads, as we have described. Each monad is filled with perceptions of the other monads, in varying degrees of clarity and distinctness. The monad's perceptions are ordered in a sequence – they perceive one state of the universe, and *then* another, and *then* another and so on – but they have no size or shape and are not located in space. At each moment, they perceive what is happening in all the other monads at that moment – and this perception of many different events at once, according to Leibniz, is what gives rise to the perception of space and a plurality of objects in space. The spatial world is the upper level in Leibniz's metaphysics, where we find infinitely divisible bodies moving around and colliding in accordance with the laws of nature and so on.

It would not be correct to think of bodies as *composed* of monads in the way that sandcastles are composed of sand; as we have said, the monads are not located in any space whatsoever. Rather, bodies *arise* out of the perceptions of the monads. A more helpful analogy to have in mind is one with the worldwide web. We can all talk about visiting "sites" on the web and discovering new "places" on the web and navigating our way through "cyberspace". But the web is not a real physical territory; it rides upon the representational states of thousands of individual computers, and has no existence apart from them. We travel through it and find places in it, but it is not in our space. Similarly, the extended world, according to Leibniz, exists through the coordinated representations of individual entities which themselves are not parts of the extended world. Our so-called "real" world of space and bodies is the virtual one generated by the monads. Our space and the entities in it gain their reality through the relations among the perceptions of the monads.

In a certain respect, this claim should be familiar. Each human being has a unique perspective upon the world of objects: for example, you see the garden from one angle, and I see it from another. Our field of perceptions is quite different, but there are structural similarities. Perhaps you and I both perceive the beets as closer to the potatoes than to the beans, although you are closer to the beans and I am closer to the potatoes. From the agreements among our perceptions we can speak sensibly of the garden of objects in a way that is neutral between our perceptions. Out of our perspectives, we construct the world that is "out there", existing independently of your perspective or my perspective. Now we may call the world out there "the real world", but Leibniz reverses this order (as did the British idealist, George Berkeley 1685–1753). The perceptions in our soul are more real than the world we construct from them, according to Leibniz. The world "out there" is an entity whose existence rides upon our perceptions. This, again, is not to say it is an illusion; it is just a second-floor phenomenon, instead of a first-floor reality. And, it must be remembered, Leibniz does not limit this view just to conscious human beings; there is an infinite set of monads perceiving the universe, one for every point in space.

How might the representations of a bunch of immaterial monads give rise to the phenomenon of a spatial world? To be sure, any adequate account of Leibniz's answer to this question would require a long book (if, that is, an adequate answer is possible at all). But we can put together a quick and inadequate sketch, for our purposes. Suppose, for simplicity's sake, there are just three monads in the universe: A, B and C. Each of them perceives the others, in varying degrees of clarity. Let us represent the degrees of clarity in their perceptions of one another by using different kinds of typeface as follows (listing the perceptions from clearest to least clear): A, A, **a**, a. Now suppose our three monads have the following sets of perceptions:

$A = \{A, b, c\}$
$B = \{a, B, C\}$
$C = \{a, B, C\}$

leibniz's world of monads   113

We can turn this information into a model of how these monads are spatially related to one another (assuming, just for this illustration, that the closer two monads are to one another, the more clearly they perceive one another). Note, first of all, that each monad perceives itself most clearly. Also, note that any two monads perceive one another with equal clarity. Note that B and C perceive one another fairly clearly, so they would be relatively close to one another. Indeed, they must be closer to one another than either is to A, since they perceive one another more clearly than either perceives A. B does perceive A just a bit more clearly than C does, so B must be closer to A than C is. With all this in mind, we can construct the following spatial model of these monads' perceptions:

A   B   C

The point of this illustration is just to show the sort of way in which non-spatial information might get turned into spatial information. In general, the illustration would not work as an explanation of Leibniz's monadic metaphysics. For one thing, there are many more than just three monads. Each monad at any time is perceiving a vast infinity of other monads, all with varying degrees of clarity. Second, the differences in degrees of clarity should not be understood always to stand for differences in spatial distance. Monads can have many different kinds of relations to one another, including relations of dominance and of greater or lesser perfection, and the clarity in a monad's perceptions may stand for one of these other relations. (As we shall soon see, monads that enter into the composition of an animal's body will have a clearer perception of the animal's "dominant" monad that they will of one another, even if the parts of the body they help to compose are very close to one another.) So distance is not the only thing, or even the main thing. Finally, for all we know, Leibniz may have meant for "spatiality" to be already built into the perceptions of each monad, in the way that your thought of a soccer field has some spatiality already built into it. Maybe he did; maybe he did not. All in all, Leibniz did not provide a detailed account of exactly how or why the spatial world arises out of the world of monadic perceptions. This sketch is meant only to provide some encouragement for his basic line of thought, that an ordered series of perceptions in non-spatial substances can in fact support a spatial model for those perceptions.

Motivation: simplicity

Despite some affinity with our ordinary notions of individual perspectives, it must be admitted that this is an outlandish and even bizarre metaphysical view. What could possibly motivate it? As we shall see, the view has the benefit of deftly ducking a range of philosophical problems, such as the problem of causality and the mind–body problem. But perhaps the most important philosophical doctrine driving Leibniz's metaphysics is the view that real substances must be *simple*.

A substance, in anyone's metaphysics, is a principal player in the universe. Ultimately, the truths of the universe must be translatable into truths about the universe's ultimate entities, which are the universe's substances. Now, can a substance be composed of other things? It seems that it cannot. For if a substance were composed of other things, then these other things would be the true substances. A substance, if it is a true substance, must not be composed of more basic things – and that is to say that a substance must be simple.

Let us next ask if a substance can have size. Again, it seems that it cannot. For if it did, it would have parts: a right half and a left half, an inside and an outside. But substances are simple, and have no parts. Therefore (Leibniz concluded) substances must be sizeless, or non-extended.

Then what is a substance, if it is not extended? If we follow Descartes and Spinoza, we shall believe that there are only two attributes we can conceive, thought and extension. If a substance is not extended, then it is a mind, or at least mind-like. A Cartesian mind is non-extended and without parts, but it is also capable of existing in various *states*, such as the state of *solving* an algebraic equation or *contemplating* metaphysical truths or *wondering* whether one's patron will come through with the cash. These states are representational and can be extremely detailed and complex. Leibniz modelled his monads on Cartesian minds, as substances that are non-extended and simple, with states that can represent complex objects.

Leibniz believes that there must be fundamental substances in the universe. Of course, this is not to say that there must be atoms, or unbreakable subatomic particles. As we shall see, Leibniz believed that the world of bodies is divisible without limit. Instead, Leibniz believes that there must be a "basement" to reality, some fundamental entities that provide the most basic facts about the world. The monads are the entities that allow for the possibility of ultimate explanations – everything in our phenomenal world is explained ultimately by what they do, and what they do is not explained in terms of any more fundamental substances. They are the ontological bedrock of our universe.

> **KEY POINTS**
>
> - Leibniz believed that the spatiotemporal world is somehow generated by an infinite population of simple, immaterial substances called "monads". Each monad contains within itself representations of all other monads, from a distinctive point of view.
> - The monads are "windowless" in the sense that no information enters them or leaves them. Each is entirely pre-programmed with all of its perceptions.
> - The monads' perceptions are perfectly coordinated in a universal harmony.

Problems solved: causality, and mind–body

By making monads "windowless" – that is, nothing enters into them or exits from them – Leibniz also answered the problem of causality. If we recall our earlier discussion of occasionalism in Chapter 1, we shall remember that seventeenth-century philosophers were puzzled over how one thing can exert causal influence upon another. Motion, for example, is a property of a body, and properties cannot be passed from one substance to another; so it seems that bodies cannot pass motion to one another (this is the problem of body–body causation). So the occasionalists believed that God miraculously brings about changes to bodies on the occasions of their collisions with other bodies, making it seem as if bodies actually affect one another when really they do not.

Leibniz was sensitive to the problem of causation, but he recoiled from the suggestion that God has his finger in every apparent instance of causation. So he concluded instead that monads chug along from representational state to representational state entirely on their own, without being affected in any way by other monads. Each monad at any particular time is in some state; it is armed at the same time with a rule or formula determining its next state; and from that state there is a rule determining its next state, and so on. But the monads are not all chugging along in arbitrary and uncoordinated ways. They have been synchronized and coordinated by God in such a way that they agree with one another in their representations. Leibniz calls this a *universal harmony* among the monads – they are all set to bring about the right sets of representations at the right times so as to make it seem as if there is a universe of entities in causal interaction with one another. God stacks the deck, so to speak.

This allows for an easy solution to the mind–body problem. Each human being has a soul and a body. The soul is a monad that is our consciousness, just as a Cartesian dualist believes. The body, as we have seen, is a phenomenon arising out of a complex set of relations among an infinite number of monads. The two of them are perfectly coordinated through God's pre-established harmony, so that my decision to raise my arm is coordinated with my arm rising, and the collision of my toe with a stone is coordinated with my perception of pain. Mind and body appear to interact, just as colliding billiard balls appear to interact, but in both cases it is a matter of God planting a synchronized agreement among the perceptions of the monads.

The universal harmony among monadic perceptions is thorough enough and precise enough to allow for a purely mechanical account of worldly phenomena (setting aside biblical miracles for the moment). That is to say, Leibniz believed that a physicist armed with all the data and the right mechanical laws of nature could explain and predict all natural events with perfect accuracy. Moreover, Leibniz believed that bodies affect one another only through collision; action at a distance, such as Newtonian gravity, is not possible in Leibniz's physics. So we can say that, at the upper level of Leibniz's metaphysics, causal determinism among substances is true; at the basic level, though, there is no causal interaction among substances. Again: at the upper level, bodies affect one another only through impact, and at the basic level, substances are completely isolated from one another.

If our souls are monads, and monads mirror the rest of the universe, we might wonder why it is that we do not have many more perceptions than we in fact have. Why are we not aware of everything going on in the universe? Leibniz would say that we *do* in fact have these perceptions – but we simply are not conscious of them. It is just like when we hear a wave crash upon the shore; we must hear the splash of each drop within the wave, in some sense, but the sounds all become confused into a single crash, so that we cannot make out the component sounds with any clarity. Similarly, we perceive the whole universe from our own points of view ("however confusedly", as Leibniz says), with every event in the universe folding into the sum of our experience at any instant.

Organisms in the physical world

We have been leaning heavily upon a distinction between the basic level and the upper level in Leibniz's metaphysics. When we closely examine Leibniz's account of physical bodies, the two levels draw closer together.

Leibniz recognized that monads are very much like Cartesian minds or souls. But he also allowed that not all monads are equal in their perfections. God, for instance, is a very atypical monad, with perfectly clear perceptions of everything going on throughout the universe. God is also the only monad with the power to create or annihilate another monad. Human minds are monads capable of deliberating over courses of action and contemplating metaphysical truths. The minds of animals are monads capable of experiencing basic passions and forming memories of experiences. At the lowest end of the scale, we shall find monads that are at least capable of representing the rest of the universe, though without being in any way conscious of these perceptions. All of these monads are in varying degrees mind-like. Our universe rides upon an infinite sea of souls.

Leibniz integrated this metaphysical conclusion ("souls everywhere") with his view of the nature of physical things ("organisms everywhere"). We should remember that Leibniz lived in an age when increasingly powerful microscopes were being developed, and there appeared to be living things at every scale, in every drop of water. Leibniz drew the conclusion that we shall find organisms at every scale in nature, from the largest to the smallest. Even when we think we have something inorganic, like a brick, Leibniz supposes that upon closer examination we shall find that in fact it is composed of many tiny living things, and those things of even smaller living things, and so on without end. Leibniz wrote:

> Each portion of matter can be conceived as a garden full of plants, and as a pond full of fish. But each branch of a plant, each limb of an animal, each drop of its humors, is still another such garden or pond. (M: §67)

Following the great seventeenth-century Dutch microscopist Anton van Leeuwenhoek, let us call these tiny living organisms "animalcules". Each of these animalcules has a soul, or a single monad which brings organic unity to it. This *dominant monad* (as Leibniz called it) is the one that is most clearly represented by all the monads which give rise to the animalcule's body. It is their "celebrity" monad, so to speak: the one all the others are closely watching, and the one from which they take their cues. Now Leibniz further believes (and this, be forewarned, gets a little dizzying) that absolutely every monad is the dominant monad of some animalcule. So every monad is a soul-like being, attached to its own corporeal body, which itself rides upon an infinity of monads, each of which is a soul attached to a different corporeal body, *ad infinitum*. Every region of space, no matter how small, arises from an infinite menagerie of souls, presiding over tiny living bodies. Van Leeuwenhoek is said to have exclaimed that he found a zoo in his mouth; "Your mouth is a universe of zoos", Leibniz might have replied.

Minds and bodies

But although the physical world is a jungle teeming with animalcules, Leibniz refused to believe that minds could be explained through any branch of physical science. He believed that every physical action could be explained mechanistically – including arm raisings, puzzled expressions, head scratching, and even the delivery of long philosophical lectures. But the inward dimension of those physical actions – genuine thinking, puzzlement, discovery of belief and so on – is irreducibly mental, he believed, and there is no way that a science of nature can account for it.

Leibniz supported this belief by offering a thought-experiment. Suppose that a human's nervous system could be greatly enlarged to the size of a mill, so that we could enter into it and look around. We would see many ingenious biochemical mechanisms, but we would not see anything in it that suggested there was any thought taking place, let alone what the content of the thought was. The mental world is *ineluctably subjective*, which is to say that there is no way to get at it and explain it by looking at the surface phenomena, that is, the upper metaphysical level. Minds exist at the basic level, where the monads are, and so they cannot be explained through the complex interactions of bodies.

So in that sense what is going on in minds is quite distinct from what is going on in bodies. But in another sense there is a tight connection between the two. Leibniz believed that each monad is always related to some body (that is, to a set of monads giving rise to a body). When an animalcule dies, the soul or dominant monad ceases to be the "king" of that particular set of monads; but as the body decays and disintegrates into legions of smaller animalcules, each and every monad continues to be the king of some set of monads, or the soul of some body. Leibniz refused to call this a "transmigration" of souls – the souls do not pop into other worlds, or become attached to greater or lesser bodies on the basis of their previous lives – but he did call it a kind of transformation, in which what was once a soul of one body naturally becomes the soul of another.

This could be quite often a disappointment, especially in the case of humans. When humans die, their situation is just like the situation of plants and animals when they die: the dominant monad becomes associated with other monads, and those other monads may be conspiring to produce a body no more glorious than that of a maggot or a bacterium. This makes for an inglorious afterlife – were it not for the Christian assurance, which Leibniz took quite seriously, that at some future time our bodies will be resurrected, and our minds will once again be their kings, and we shall not die again.

KEY POINTS

- Leibniz's universal harmony solves at least two major philosophical problems (the mind–body problem and the problem of causality). Substances do not really interact: they are perfectly synchronized in such a way so as to *appear* to interact.
- Each individual body is generated by a set of monads, each of which reflects most clearly and distinctly one particular monad (the dominant monad).
- Moreover, each and every monad is the dominant monad of some body.
- The physical world is composed of an infinity of "animalcules" – organisms within organisms, without end.
- Monads never die, but over time they come to be associated with different bodies.

Truth as containment, and complete concepts

Because each monad is a world unto itself, with no real connection to any other created monad, Leibniz has to explain exactly what makes claims about the phenomenal world true. Normally when we have a true claim such as "The donkey is in the garden," what makes it true is its connection to a set of circumstances (in this case, the presence of a donkey in the garden). But, of course, at the basic level of Leibnizian metaphysics, there are no donkeys or gardens, only sets of monads giving rise to them. So how does Leibniz account for truth? Perhaps Leibniz could have done so by appealing to what must be going on in monads in order to give rise to the relevant sets of circumstances – thus what makes "The donkey is in the garden" true is a very complex (indeed, infinitely complex) configuration of monadic perceptions, which when taken together constitute the fact of there being a donkey in the garden. But he had a more elegant route available to him. All we need to do is focus on the dominant monad of the subject of the claim (in this case, the donkey). That monad, like any monad, mirrors the rest of the universe. And so, to account for the truth of the "The donkey is in the garden," we need only indicate that the predicate of the claim – *being in the garden* – is present in the dominant monad's perception of its own situation. If it is present, then the claim is true; if not, it is false.

The quick way of saying this is to say that all truths are analytic, according to Leibniz. Every true claim is true because the predicate of the claim is *contained* within the subject. We can see what this means by turning towards the kinds of claims that most philosophers have thought to be analytic. "A triangle has three sides," for example, is usually considered to be analytic, since having three sides is simply part of what it is to be a triangle. That is what it means to say the predicate is contained within the subject: having that predicate is part of what it is to be that subject. The predicate in analytic truths does not really tell us anything new, since once we know what a triangle is, anyone can readily see that any triangle has three sides.

Now most philosophers recognize that at least *some* truths are analytic – the ones that seem automatically true, or true by definition, such as "My father's brother is my uncle". Leibniz, though, makes the huge claim that *all* truths are analytic. "The donkey is in the garden," if true at all, is true in just the same way that "A triangle has three sides" is true. It is true because once we unpack what it really means to be the donkey in question – with the way that the monad associated with that donkey mirrors the rest of the universe – we shall readily see that it is in the garden. Part of what it is to be that donkey is for it to be in that garden, at least for part of its life.

Leibniz was able to get away with making this radical pronouncement because he invests so much in every single monad. Indeed, he said that there is correlated with each monad a *complete concept* of the entity for whom that monad is the dominant one, and included in such a complete concept is everything that is, was or will be true of that entity. So, to switch to one of Leibniz's own examples, the complete concept of Julius Caesar includes where he was born, who his parents were, every fact of his adolescence, his military campaigns, his assassination and so on. If we wondered what makes it true that Caesar crossed the Rubicon river in 49 BC, all we need to know is that in the long list of everything contained within the complete concept of Julius Caesar ("the man who was born in 102 BC, fought in the Gallic wars, . . . , crossed the Rubicon into Italy in 49 BC, . . . defeated Pompey, was assassinated in 44 BC") there is one relevant entry that makes it true; and thus crossing the Rubicon is just as much part of what it is to be Julius Caesar as it is part of a triangle to have three sides.

In one of his essays, "Primary Truths", Leibniz attempts to show how most of the fundamental features of his metaphysics (containment, the isolation of monads, universal harmony, the transformation of organisms, and more) all follow from the conviction that all truths are analytic. It is thus a central fixture in his metaphysics.

Puzzles about contingency

But if every truth about every subject is analytically true, just as "A triangle has three sides" is analytically true, does that make every truth as necessary and inevitable as any geometrical truth? That is, if everything Julius Caesar ever does is automatically true of him, is there any sense in which Caesar could ever be free to do something else?

This is an extremely important question for Leibniz; he worked as hard to fend off necessity as he worked on anything else in his life. We have seen how he loathed Spinoza's metaphysics, with its necessitarianism and its impersonal deity. He had to find a way to preserve contingency (that is, the non-necessity of some things) while maintaining the containment theory of truth, which was central to his metaphysical vision of the world. The full account of Leibniz's response will take us into another major doctrine in Leibniz's metaphysics, the doctrine of possible worlds. But before getting into that, we can make some headway on this question by exploring Leibniz's claim that the distinction between necessary and contingent truths really comes down to the distinction between what is provable and what is not.

We can begin by considering the kinds of claims Leibniz would have regarded as necessarily true. These are the claims of logic (such as if both A and B are true, then A is true), the claims of arithmetic (such as 2 + 3 = 5), the claims of geometry (like our triangle example), the claims of metaphysics (such as that substances are simple) and also some basic truths about physics (such as the claim that two bodies cannot share the same space). No one, not even God, has any choice about whether these claims are true; they simply have to be true, given the meanings of their terms, and the nature of reason, quantity, space and body. No two ways about it. But other claims – such as that there is a donkey in the garden, or that Leibniz's father died when he was six – do not seem as if they are necessarily true. The universe had some choice about these, it seems; things could have been otherwise. These claims are contingent, not necessary.

Now, what accounts for the difference between necessary and contingent truths? Leibniz's containment theory of truth offers no help, for all true claims are true in virtue of their predicates being included in their subjects. But Leibniz said that we can generate the same difference by asking whether the truths can be proven in a finite number of steps: all necessary truths can be so proven, Leibniz says, and the contingent ones cannot. If we take as our example "2 + 3 = 5", we might try to prove it as follows:

1. $2 =_{df} 1 + 1$
2. $3 =_{df} 1 + 1 + 1$
3. $5 =_{df} 1 + 1 + 1 + 1 + 1$
4. So (from 1 and 2), $2 + 3 = 1 + 1 + 1 + 1 + 1$
5. But then it follows (from 3 and 4) that $2 + 3 = 5$.

That is the idea, anyway: that a necessary truth can be proven crisply in a finite series of numbered steps, where each step is a definition or something that results from substituting equals for equals. But we cannot do this when it comes to contingent truths such as "The donkey is in the garden". Suppose we try:

1. Donkey = $_{df}$ hoofed, herbivorous mammal with long ears
2. Garden = $_{df}$ plot of ground for growing fruit, flowers or vegetables
3. . . . ?

We get stuck at step 3 because there is nothing in the definitions of "donkey" and "garden" to suggest any chain of substitutions that will result in the conclusion that some particular donkey is in the garden. The concept of a particular donkey (as opposed to the concept of donkeys in general) is infinitely complex, since it includes within it relations to everything else in its universe. It is because of this infinite complexity that contingent truths cannot be proven in the same crisp way that necessary truths can be proven. Indeed, in the end, the only way to prove that a particular contingent truth is true is by proving that it is a truth in a world which, when compared to all other possible worlds, turns out to be the best. (We shall examine this claim shortly.)

So Leibniz proposed reducing one distinction (necessary versus contingent) to another (provable versus not provable). But even if the two distinctions do indeed line up perfectly – and who is to say if they do? – it is still not clear what Leibniz thought he had accomplished. Why should it matter whether a true statement can be crisply proven if it is still nevertheless true that its subject contains its predicate? Why should a statement's unprovability make it contingent? It is not perfectly clear how Leibniz would answer these questions, but we know that his answer would have something to do with his belief that contingent truths depend for their truth on God's choice to actualize this world as opposed to any other possible world. We turn next to Leibniz's doctrine of possible worlds.

Possible worlds

For the moment (and without letting this go to your head), put yourself in God's situation before the creation of the world. You are inclined towards creating something. But what should you create? You have many options, from the creation of a single lonely lepton to the creation of galaxies filled with choirs of angels, and so on without end. There is an infinite array of possible universes you can create. But you are an infinitely powerful, infinitely knowledgeable and perfectly benevolent being, and you understand that for each and every possible thing, that thing would prefer its existence to its nonexistence; in a slogan, "all things strive toward existence". And so you incline towards creating a maximal world – a world with as many different possible things packed into it as can be packed together without contradiction (for you are a rational deity). Moreover, you want this world to show the greatest splendour – the variety among the different things in the world must be as great as possible. And you want this splendour to be displayed with the greatest possible harmony and continuity: the world should be an aesthetic masterpiece, with a simple set of laws binding together the world's diversity, and with a plethora of intermediate creatures plugging the gaps between the major species. You are also a perfectly just deity, and so you would wish your creation to exhibit justice without exception. No good deed will go unrewarded, and no evil deed will go unpunished. In short, you are inclined to create the best world out of all possible worlds, where "best" is measured in *every* available dimension: completeness, greatness, splendour, beauty, harmony, continuity and justice. Only such a creation would be worthy of your perfect nature.

It is just such a world that Leibniz believed God to have created. Indeed, once it is agreed that there is a god who has created the world, and that God has all those wonderful features like omnipotence and omniscience, what other world would God create? The actual world – *our* world – must be the best of all possible worlds, since God created it, and it must exhibit all of the features we have articulated. This "science" of all the considerations that go into the creation of the best of all possible worlds is what Leibniz calls *theodicy*.

From this theodicy we can learn of many features of our world, Leibniz believed. We know that there will be justice, sooner or later, and that the overall tilt of the world is in favour of goodness and pleasure. We know that in nature we shall find no sudden leaps between species or between events; nature moves in infinite gradations from one thing to another, letting everything along the way into existence. And we know that the world will be governed by a single set of harmonious laws, as the work of God must be a beautiful and elegant artefact.

Leibniz believed that the other possible worlds exist as ideas within God's understanding. They are blueprints for worlds he could have created. Many of these worlds are worlds in which Julius Caesar did not cross the Rubicon – because he stayed out of Italy, or was never born, or died as a child, or whatever. God *could* have created any of these worlds. But God was "infallibly inclined" to create the best possible world, and that is what exists. And so, Leibniz says, it is true that Caesar could have refrained from crossing the Rubicon – that is to say, God could have created a world in which someone very much like our Caesar did not cross the Rubicon.

This, at last, might provide the link between contingency and unprovability. Any contingent truth is one that is true in some but not all possible worlds. (The necessary truths are true in all possible worlds, since it is not possible for them to be false.) In order to provide a crisp, logical proof for a contingent truth, one would have to demonstrate that the truth is part and parcel of the best of all possible worlds.

Perhaps Leibniz's thought is that this demonstration would require an infinite number of steps, since it would require that we show that the actual world is better than possible world number 2, and better than possible world number 3, and better than . . .

> **KEY POINTS**
> - For each substance, there is a complete concept of that substance, a concept which includes every truth about that substance.
> - This makes every truth *analytic*, meaning that anything truly said of a subject is part of the concept of that subject.
> - Some truths are necessary (must be true) and some are contingent (could have been otherwise). One way of capturing this difference, according to Leibniz, is to see whether the truth can be proven in a finite number of steps. If it can, the truth is necessary; if not, it is contingent.
> - There are infinitely many other possible worlds God could have created. God was infallibly inclined (though not necessitated) to create the very best one, which is this world.

God

At this point we may wish to back up and ask some more basic questions. Just how does Leibniz know that there is a God, and that God created the world? Leibniz's "official" argument for God's existence is the ontological argument, which purports to show that God, by his very nature, must exist. God is understood to be the being that is absolutely perfect – that is, the being with all "perfections", where perfections are understood to be pure and simple positive qualities. One such perfection is existence itself: existence is a power some possible things (like reindeer) possess, and other possible things (like unicorns) lack. God, as the being with all perfections, must possess it. Therefore, God necessarily exists.

This ontological argument had been offered in various forms by philosophers before Leibniz (such as Anselm, Descartes and Spinoza), although Leibniz seems to have been the first to recognize that along with this proof one must also show that God is a genuinely possible being – that is, that it is possible for one single being to possess all perfections (they do not run against one another). Leibniz attempts to prove this by reasoning that each perfection is pure and simple – it cannot be analysed into components. If this is true, then it seems that no contradiction could ever be derived by positing the existence of two perfections: there would not be enough "there" in each perfection to contradict or disallow the positing of the other perfection.

A more interesting and original argument for God's existence can be found within Leibniz's *Monadology*. There Leibniz argues that if there are essences – pure concepts discoverable through logic, mathematics and metaphysics, which express possible beings or truths – then there must be a being that *grounds* those essences. There must be a being in whom these essences exist, and this being is God.

> This is because God's understanding is the realm of eternal truths or that of the ideas on which they depend; without him there would be nothing real in possibles, and not only would nothing exist, but also nothing would be possible.
> (M: §67)

Leibniz's observation is that we must explain the existence of essences if we are to speak and think validly about what *could* be true, and what *could not* be true. The greatest examples of our conceptual knowledge are found in mathematics and logic, and these sciences are purely conceptual in nature, and rule with certainty about what is possible and what is not. Yet the truths of mathematics and logic are not grounded in material things such as stone and lumber; they are grounded in pure concepts. What makes these concepts real? Leibniz's answer is that their reality must be due to a being whose existence is necessary, and whose resources allow for the expression of every possible thing: God. Thus God is the guarantor of our conceptual knowledge.

This argument gets to the heart of what any rationalist wants from God. God serves as the substance that underwrites the rationalists' intellectual discoveries. Plato posited a final form, the form of the good, which in some sense lent being to all the other forms and secured the validity of his own dialectical reasoning. Descartes, Spinoza and Leibniz all seek the same from their respective gods.

Once we are assured of the existence of a being with all perfections who grounds the very possibility of all possible things, it is but a short step to assure oneself that this being is responsible for the reality of our world. If we know God exists, and we know God to be the being in virtue of whom all things are possible, then we know that the existence of every actual thing depends ultimately upon the existence of God.

Key points

- According to Leibniz, our physical world is an apparent one, generated by a world of simple, immaterial monads, perfectly coordinated in their perceptions.
- These monads are souls, which come to be associated with different apparent bodies over time.
- God chose to actualize this collection of monads, over infinitely many other possible ones, because it gives rise to the best possible world.
- God exists necessarily, and the mind of God is the foundation for all of our concepts.

six
Leibniz's justice and freedom

The ethics of creation

As we saw in Chapter 5, Leibniz believes that God grounds the possibility of all things, and is responsible for turning our world from a merely possible world into the actual one. Out of all possible worlds, God chose this one to be real. Why this one? Leibniz's answer, of course, is that this is the *best* of all possible worlds: it offers the widest diversity of phenomena, the simplest and most elegant set of natural laws, complete justice and consummate moral perfection. This may not seem to us to be so, of course, given our limited and fragmented experience. But, Leibniz would say, if we could survey the entire scope of our world, including what goes on in the afterlife, we would see that no better world is possible.

This provides a broad target for ridicule. Indeed, the French philosopher Voltaire (1694–1778) devotes his entire novel, *Candide*, to ridiculing it. Voltaire introduces Dr Pangloss, a fool of a philosopher who goes to absurd lengths to try to show a divine purpose in every awful atrocity. Earthquakes, rape, murder, torture and disease – Pangloss tries to argues that all these horrors must be present for the world to be as "wonderful" as it is. The end result is sickening: for how can anyone witness the death of a child and proudly assert that all is for the best? At the same time, though, it must be remembered that Leibniz himself lived in the midst of one of Europe's bloodiest wars. He knew well the range of human atrocity. Yet he drew his conclusion based on his unshakeable conviction that God must exist, and that God could not possibly create anything less than the best. Leibniz surely would not have offered Pangloss's trite justifications; but he might have stood alongside the victims and counselled, "This may be unthinkable to you now, but I promise you that there will be a day when you are able to see God's love even in this." Extraordinary optimism, to be sure. But at the same time, it may be the only way to reconcile deep tragedy with faith in a beneficent God.

Leibniz rarely argued from what we see to conclusions about God. It is true that the natural world filled him with admiration and wonder, and he saw plenty of confirming evidence for his conclusion that God created the world. But his certainty of God's existence and beneficence was justified by *a priori* arguments – that is, arguments based on the resources of reason alone. That being said, in one instance he did allow his experience to tell him something about God. Leibniz's experience taught him that the demands of justice are rarely met in this world: we see the guilty go unpunished, and the just are not rewarded. From this he concluded that there *must* be a life after this life, a life in which justice is served. For Leibniz understood the demands of justice to be as inviolable as any metaphysical laws. Even God, he said, is subject to them.

Metaphysical perfectionism

To make sense of Leibniz's account of justice, we first need to understand the notion of metaphysical perfection. Although they rarely made it explicit, all of the seventeenth-century rationalists had such a notion and put it to use in their metaphysical systems. (One aspect of metaphysical perfectionism has been discussed in the introduction to this volume, as the "gradations of reality" thesis.) In rough, the notion is that things come in varying degrees of "perfection" or "reality". "Perfection" here should be understood as a synonym for "completeness" or "fullness". Completeness or fullness of what? Of *being*. God, as one would expect, is the most real or most perfect thing. A finite thing such as a human being has less reality or perfection. A mere quality (such as *being round*) has even less. And *nothing*, of course, has no perfection or reality whatsoever.

This is a curious notion, made all the more curious to us by the fact that we do not share it. We think of an entity as real, or not. And we think of an entity as being perfect in some respect (e.g. perfectly round, etc.) or not. It is puzzling to conceive of reality or perfection or completeness as varying in degrees. It would be nice to have a better understanding of this theory, but none of the rationalists offers a careful explication of it; they all seem to rely on it and take it as somewhat obvious. But from what they say, and some speculation, we can offer two observations that shed some light on the idea.

First, reality/perfection seems to correlate to ontological self-sufficiency – or, in other words, independent existence. God is wholly self-sufficient, requiring no other thing in order to exist. A finite substance, though, is not wholly self-sufficient, since it needs God's concurrence in order to exist. But a finite substance does have more independence than a mere quality, since a mere quality needs not only God's concurrence, but also some thing to belong to. So, basically, the greater a thing's perfection/reality, the less the thing's reliance upon other entities for its existence.

Second – and for our purposes here, more importantly – existent things all consist of varying degrees of ingredients that we might say belong on "the periodic table of perfections". The analogy with the periodic table of the elements is meant to suggest that, according to metaphysical perfectionism, all entities are constituted by various perfections in various degrees. So, for example, let us suppose that power, knowledge and freedom are all perfections. A human is constituted by a certain degree of power, a certain degree of knowledge and (perhaps) a certain degree of freedom. A sloth also has these perfections, but to far lesser degrees. God, at the upper limit, is the being constituted by all perfections, each to an unlimited degree. It is in this sense that we can think of finite beings as approximations of God – they share God's perfections, but unlike God they have only limited degrees of these perfections.

(What counts as a perfection? Again, no one has offered a comprehensive list, but we can speculate that a property is a perfection if it is *qualitative*, not quantitative; a *proficiency*, not a deficiency; and if it can be *possessed in its entirety*. Knowledge, for example, is a quality of a mind; and it is a positive quality, not a deficiency; and it seems that an entity could possess all knowledge, if the entity were omniscient. Physical size, by contrast, is quantitative in nature, and there is no biggest size a thing can have, so size is not a perfection. This account is by no means complete, and leaves many questions unanswered – is power really *qualitative* as opposed to quantitative? Why should *circularity* not count as a perfection? – but it does reflect what little the rationalists have to say about perfections.)

Thus, according to metaphysical perfectionism, we can place all beings somewhere on a scale of perfection, or a "chain of being", with

God and the top and *nothing* at the bottom. Descending from God we find perhaps angels, and then humans, and then non-rational animals, and plants, and inanimate objects. They share in various degrees in the perfections that God possesses in their entirety; creatures are "godly" in varying degrees. *Imperfection*, on this view, is not a real feature that a thing possesses, but a lack of something real, a *lack* of a perfection. And it is crucial to Leibniz's moral theory that there is an objective truth about a thing's degree of perfection. The truth about whether one thing is more perfect than another is not relative to person, time or culture. A thing's degree of perfection is a real fact about that thing, which we can discover through our wisdom.

Charity of the wise

Leibniz believes that one ought to love something in proportion to that thing's metaphysical perfection – that is, according to the thing's position on the great chain of being. Of course, in order to accurately discern a thing's perfection, one must have a kind of wisdom. And so, for Leibniz, morality comes down to the love a wise person would bestow upon things. This is Leibniz's understanding of justice: justice is the *charity* (or "love") of the wise.

Now what is the strength of the "ought" here? Why *should* we love things in proportion to their perfection? Leibniz's "ought" seems to be based on two considerations. First, Leibniz thinks that, simply as a matter of fact, we *do* take great pleasure in the perception of perfections, and so we automatically love things to the extent that we recognize perfections in them. This is simply a psychological fact about beings with intellects. As a mere psychological fact, it does not really give us a reason for thinking that we *ought* to love perfect things; for all we know this fact about us might be totally irrelevant to what we ought to do. But this psychological fact does play a central role in the next consideration.

The second consideration is that the "ought" is motivated by a kind of selfish concern for pleasure. If we are interested in enjoying the deepest and most powerful pleasure – and Leibniz would say that this surely does interest us – then we should seek out the things with the highest degrees of perfection and take pleasure in them and love them accordingly. "Love", Leibniz writes, "is that mental state which makes us take pleasure in the perfections of the object of our love" (PW: 83). Now

Leibniz would admit that pleasures can be deceptive. We often do not perceive things adequately, and sometimes we feel pleasure in something that later brings about a great deal of suffering, or brings about a lesser state of perfection in us. For this reason he says we should be wary of the pleasures of the senses, regarding them like "flattering enemies", since they so often contain within themselves the seeds of greater imperfection. But through the use of our reason we can become better at distinguishing wholesome pleasures from destructive ones, and in so doing we grow in wisdom. In this, Leibniz agrees with both Descartes and Spinoza: reason allows us to distinguish the true pleasures and joys from those with only shiny packaging.

We take pleasure in feeling perfection in ourselves, as when we grow in knowledge or power or wisdom. And we also take pleasure in just the same way when we see perfection in other beings, as when we contemplate God or witness another's growth in some perfection. So while Leibniz thinks our obligation to love other things is rooted in a selfish desire for our own pleasure, at the same time he holds that we gain pleasure in others' perfection, even if that perfection does not directly benefit us in any other way. When I witness another person exercising their wisdom in making a decision, for example, I gain pleasure in seeing this, even when the decision does not concern me at all. So we take genuine joy in the level of others' perfection, and that is the ground for our love for them. And we find the greatest joy in the contemplation of God's perfection, and not because of any expectation of what God might do for us. We simply are thrilled to see the fullness and perfection, whether it is in us or in another.

Thus the central moral task we face is to gain a proper understanding of the relative perfection of things, and to love them in proportion to their perfection. This extends to things, as when we prefer one better work of art to a lesser one. It also extends to people, as when we reward someone for a wise decision or punish someone for being a fool. And it extends also to actions, when we see that one course of action would be wiser than an alternative. Leibniz writes,

> Justice is charity or a habit of loving conformed to wisdom. Thus when one is inclined toward justice, one tries to procure good for everybody, so far as one can, reasonably, but in proportion to the needs and merits of each: and even if one is obliged sometimes to punish evil persons, it is for the general good. (PW: 83)

In short, in all our judgements we should incline towards the better or best, just as God does in creating our world. Like God, we seek to bring about the best of all possible worlds, so far as our powers allow.

Emulating God

We know that God, as the most perfect being, is perfect in wisdom and in love; so we know that God is perfectly just. We also know that God selected this world for creation because it is the most perfect of all possible worlds, and so God must love this world more than any other possible one. Armed with this knowledge, we can look to the world to try to gain a better understanding of perfection. That is to say, we can try to see the divine wisdom in our world. This is tricky business, to be sure, as one should not fall into Dr Pangloss's shallow optimism. But by trying to deepen our understanding of the world, while at the same time paying close attention to the pleasure we gain through that understanding, we can grow in wisdom.

So, for example, Leibniz would say that if we examine the natural world, we shall find that nature does nothing in "leaps": there is a gradual continuity among natural things, and between any two species we shall find another. From this, and the fact that God preferred this world over others, we can learn that continuity is a perfection. Perhaps this would then influence our art or politics or philosophy in some fashion, as we try to make our productions perfect in the same way that God made his production perfect. Being a student of nature is like being the student of Rembrandt or Haydn; we learn from these masters at least in part by studying the perfections of their works.

As we grow in wisdom, we can get better at choosing the courses of actions that contribute towards this being the best of all possible worlds. In this way, we assist God in creation in the sense that we help the world to become as perfect as it is as a finished product in God's mind. "The very law of justice", says Leibniz,

> wills that each one participate in the perfection of the universe and in happiness of his own, proportional to his own virtue and to the good will he entertains toward the common good, by which that which we call the charity and love of God is fulfilled, in which alone, according to the judgment of the wisest theologians, the force and power of the Christian religion itself consists. (UOT: 154)

As one might put it – though this sounds so sugary that one hesitates to say it – we are "God's little helpers", like Santa's elves, who work in accordance with God's plan to make this the best possible world. (With a little less sugar, we could call ourselves "God's lieutenants".) Just as some of today's Christians ask what Jesus would do, Leibniz suggests that we ask what God would have us do. And that is: bring about the best, from among all the various possibilities available.

Now it might be fairly complained that this does not give us much guidance, for how are we to know for sure what will bring about the most perfection? Leibniz would probably grant the objection, saying that acting with justice is just as difficult as it is valuable. But he did think a more specific moral agenda could be gathered from the perspective he offered:

> Now a good will or a rightful intention consists in . . . the love of God and one's neighbor. For that reason one must neglect nothing which serves God's honor . . . [One must] especially love justice, be hard on oneself and indulgent toward others . . . [and] always be mindful of the general good. [It is essential] . . . to speak ill of no one . . . to be helpful to everyone . . . to suffer a small misfortune sooner than to let another suffer a great misfortune, to do nothing that one would not gladly endure oneself. To give alms without ostentation; to take pity on the distressed and the unhappy, and to practice the works of charity. (PW: 107)

In short, Leibniz advocated what might be recognized as the "Christian" virtues (although of course they are also urged by many other religions as well). He did believe that through reason and wisdom we can – at least in principle – work out the right thing to do. But humans often do neglect their wisdom and reason poorly, and it is for that reason that God taught some precepts of morality through Moses, the prophets and Jesus Christ.

Leibniz would be the first to admit that, although we have in principle everything we need to be just, as a matter of fact we have fallen far short. There are imperfections in the world. This is in part an inevitable consequence of the world being populated by creatures, none of which is as perfect as God. There will be limitations and partialities that result in ignorance, pain and death. The world's imperfection is also due in part to our being unwilling to perfect our wisdom as much as we ought, and acting like fools as a consequence. Our world may be the best of all possible worlds, but that does not mean there will not be instances of malevolence, imperfection and suffering. Regarding any particular instance of evil, all we can say is that

> since God has found it good that [this instance should occur] in spite of the sin which God foresaw, this evil must be compensated for with interest in the universe and that God will draw a greater good from it and that it will turn out that this sequence of events including the existence of this [evil], is the most perfect among all other possible kinds. (DM: §30)

So, according to Leibniz, this will turn out to be the best of all possible worlds, and each of us will certainly play his or her role in helping this to become the best. Some of us will do so through acts of charity; others will do so through sins, which will afford God the opportunity to display a strict and perfect justice.

KEY POINTS

- All things are metaphysically perfect in varying degrees. The central moral task, according to Leibniz, is to love each thing in proportion to its perfection. Doing so constitutes justice.
- We can learn valuable lessons from nature about metaphysical perfection, since what we find in nature was selected by God as better than any possible alternative.
- God creates the best world out of all possible worlds. Similarly, we should emulate God in choosing the best action out of all possible actions. In doing this, we help this world to become the best of all possible worlds.

Blame

But someone might now complain that the world, as Leibniz describes it, is anything but just from the perspective of the creatures within it. God's selection of our world is based on its overall perfection, and the overall triumph of goodness over evil. Individuals contribute to this overall quality, but sometimes their contributions are quite unpleasant. Judas, for example, who betrays Jesus, suffers eternally for his sin. Leibniz assures us that somehow this feature is required in order for the world to be the best possible one – but this is of small consolation to

Judas! He pays eternally for playing his role in the big scheme of things over which he seemingly had no choice or control. Where is the justice in that?

Leibniz would insist that Judas *did* have choice or control over his actions. No one forced him into the betrayal or offered him a deal he truly could not refuse. His decision was made on the basis of his own beliefs, judgements and inclinations. It was in this sense *spontaneous* – it arose out of his own will. Moreover, the act was *intelligent* in the sense that he deliberated over it, considered reasons and made his decision. And his act was in fact *contingent* in the sense that there certainly were other possibilities available to him. Spontaneity, intelligence and contingency: these are the hallmarks of a free decision, according to Leibniz.

Still, at this point we should recall the broad reach of Leibniz's determinism. He believed that each event in the universe is determined by antecedent events and the laws of nature – and this holds for psychological events as well as physical ones. So Judas ended up with his particular beliefs, judgements and inclinations because of his given nature and the experiences he encountered. And although he did deliberate over his action, his decision was in some sense a foregone conclusion, given the psychological pressures he was under. So it is hard to see how other possibilities were really available to him. He could not have done otherwise – unless he had been a different person, or had had fundamentally different experiences. Why then should he be considered blameworthy for what he did?

There are two replies Leibniz could give to this line of objection. First, he could claim that it is wrong to think of Judas as a victim suffering from his given nature and his experiences, as if these things are alien to himself. Rather, in an important sense Judas *is* that given nature, combined with those experiences: these things are what makes him Judas. If he were to try to claim, "Do not blame me for what I did; blame it on the way I was made, and on the way the world shaped me," then he would be telling us to blame him after all, since he is nothing apart from these things. In other words, as Leibniz wrote, "Why is it that this man will assuredly commit this sin? The reply is easy: otherwise he would not be this man" (DM: §30). He would be a different man, with a different history and psychological structure. If he were to complain that he is the way he is, he would be complaining that he exists. And if he were to make this complaint, God could reply in his own defence that Judas's existence – exactly as it actually is – is a necessary component of the best of all possible worlds.

This philosophical view is known as *compatibilism*. The view is that freedom means something other than "could have done otherwise". Instead, freedom means autonomy, or being responsible yourself for the decisions you make. If your decision is made from your own beliefs, preferences, desires and goals, then it is free. It does not matter whether you could have done otherwise, given those beliefs, preferences and so on. What matters is that *you* were in charge of your decision, and no one else.

Leibniz's second reply to Judas's complaint is the one he usually offers when considering this objection. It is to remind us of the sense in which Judas indeed could have done otherwise. God could have made actual a different possible world, one in which Judas does not betray Jesus but instead lives a long and happy life by his side. That world is possible; hence it could have been true that Judas did not betray Jesus; and hence it is true that Judas could have done otherwise. Not our *actual* Judas, of course; but *another* Judas, in another world, who is very much like this Judas except for some psychological features or details in his upbringing or circumstances.

We can imagine Judas again complaining that this "could have done otherwise" applies more to God than to him: "Perhaps God could have done otherwise; but I, such as I am, cannot!" But Leibniz is offering a new and different understanding of what "could have done otherwise" really means. It does not mean that Judas had the freedom to violate the laws of nature, or somehow violate the determinism that runs through the universe. No creature has this power. To say "things could have been otherwise" is to say, rather, that another world (with other individuals) might have been actual. If Leibniz is right in this proposal about what contingency really is, then Judas is stuck with the conclusion that he could have done otherwise, whether or not it fits his own sense of "could have done otherwise".

But this favoured reply by Leibniz leads us to another very difficult question within Leibniz's philosophy: if this world is the best one, and God must do what is best, then in what sense could God have made another world actual? Are those other worlds, with other possible Judases in them, genuinely possible?

God's freedom

Leibniz tried different answers to this question over his whole intellectual life. Indeed, perhaps the philosophical principle most dear to him was the principle that Spinoza was wrong: not everything is necessary, and other possibilities are genuine possibilities. But it seems that Leibniz is very close to Spinozism unless he can find a way to deny at least one of the following claims:

1. Necessarily, God creates what is best.
2. Necessarily, this world is the best of all possible worlds.

For if those claims are both true, then it is hard to see how any other world is truly possible. Over his career, Leibniz denied each of these claims in various ways at different times in his persistent effort to hold fast to the conclusion that this world is not necessitated by God.

In some writings Leibniz denies (1), that God necessarily creates the best possible world. He claims that God *could* create a "less-than-the-best" world, or possibly no world at all. In other words, there would be no contradiction in a second-best world coming into existence: such a world is internally coherent. What keeps God from creating such a world is God's consummate goodness. God is *morally* required, one may say, to create the best possible world, but this kind of restraint is not as deep or as strong as a logical or metaphysical restraint (such as the restraint that keeps God from creating a world where two plus three does not equal five). Leibniz tries to express the difference in strength between these restraints by observing that God is not necessitated to create the best possible world, but God is "infallibly inclined" to do so. Infallible inclination – though infallible – is meant to be just a shade more forgiving than absolute necessitation. And that shade is just enough, Leibniz hoped, to keep him from falling into Spinozism. (This is the view presented in Chapter 5.)

But in other writings, Leibniz denied (2), that "This is the best possible world" is a necessary truth. He denied this not because he thought that being "best" is at all relative or arbitrary. He believed that, objectively speaking, this really is the best of all possible worlds. He only denied that this is a *necessary* fact. But what does this mean? Does it mean that – somehow – the universe of possible worlds could have been otherwise, so that some other world would have been the best?

No. Leibniz was able to deny the necessity of this world being the best only by relying upon his unique understanding of what it is for a claim to be necessary. Ordinarily we think that if a claim is necessary, then it could not have been otherwise. But, as discussed in Chapter 5, Leibniz adopts a different understanding of "necessary" which depends upon how a claim is demonstrated. If a claim can be demonstrated to be true in a finite number of steps, then it is *necessary*. If it cannot be demonstrated in a finite number of steps, it is *contingent*. Now in order to demonstrate that this is the best of all possible worlds, one would have to describe every fact and feature of this world, and show that every world in which one or more of these features were otherwise would not be as good a world as this one. This surely would require an infinite proof, given the infinity of facts about this world and the infinite number of ways in which they could be different. So it turns out to be contingent that this is the best of all possible worlds, since we cannot prove it so in a finite number of steps.

In addition to these two broad strategies of denying that this world is necessitated, Leibniz explored a range of more narrow and subtle ones as well. But for our purposes, we can say that he escaped Spinozism by two routes: (1) by claiming that God is not necessitated, but infallibly inclined to create this world, or (2) by claiming that it is only a contingent fact that this is the best world.

Judas's complaint, renewed

Still, Judas may enquire, is there any genuine sense in which he is responsible for his actions? It is perhaps true that God *could* have created another world. But even if we set aside the fact that God never *would* have created another world, it is hard to see how God's liberty in this matter means that Judas himself could have done otherwise. And it may be true that this world is the best world only contingently – but, nevertheless, this is the world that has been created, and again it is hard to see how its contingency should make Judas feel free. Maybe God could have done otherwise in one sense or another – but how could Judas have done otherwise?

In the end, Leibniz must pin his hopes upon his recommendation to understand freedom in a sense other than "could have done otherwise". Judas will sin grievously in this world – this, Leibniz admits, is certain. Judas will suffer eternal damnation for his sin – again, this is certain. We also can be certain that this divine punishment is just, and its justice requires that Judas's sin be free, not necessitated. So we must find a way for that sin to be contingent. The only route available to Leibniz – given his beliefs about God's eternality, perfection and power – is to revise our ordinary conception of what it is to be free (that is, his only route is compatibilism). We thought that freedom was the ability to do otherwise. But now we learn that an action is free when it is spontaneous, intelligent and contingent. A free action is not an undetermined one, but one determined in a certain way, out of the agent's own inner resources. And contingency, we learn, has to do with the metaphysics of God making this world actual rather than some other world, with some other Judas.

It may be that this uniquely Leibnizian account of contingency – according to which contingency is purely a matter of God's choice in creating worlds, and that it is discoverable by us in terms of whether demonstrations of true claims are finite or infinite – is hard to swallow. But, in Leibniz's defence, it should be pointed out that he was indeed wrestling with a difficult problem, reconciling the power of God with the freedom of creatures. It is fair to say that no one has worked out a solution to this problem that is not hard to swallow.

> **KEY POINTS**
> - According to Leibniz, a free choice is one that is spontaneous (meaning that the choice arises from a person's own will), intelligent and contingent. We are rightly held morally accountable for our free choices.
> - What makes a choice *contingent* for a person is the fact that God could have made actual another possible world in which that person (or someone extremely similar to him) makes a different choice.
> - What keeps God from making other possible worlds actual is God's own inclination to create the best possible world.

Why do anything?

Suppose we accept Leibniz's account, that free decisions are the ones that are spontaneous, intelligent and contingent, and that contingency resides in God's capacity to actualize some other possible world. We still might wonder how we are supposed to take our own deliberations and choices seriously, since it is nevertheless true that every action we will take is already determined to take place. Another way to put the same puzzle is this: if God has already actualized the best possible world, why exactly should we be trying to do anything, since it is a foregone conclusion that this world will turn out to be the best possible one?

This is a problem of motivation that any determinist faces. Perhaps the first thing that can be said is that although our decisions are predetermined, we simply cannot help but take them seriously when we are in the midst of making them. We are determined to view our decisions as undetermined, we might say. And it is not as if our deliberations and our decisions are unconnected: we make the decisions we do as a result of the deliberations we undergo, and so the deliberations are effective causes for our decisions. We are ignorant of what the final result will be, so we take our deliberations seriously in the hope that we will make good decisions. It may already be true that we shall make some particular decision, but since we do not now know what that decision will be, we do what we can to contribute towards it being a good decision. We cannot help but view our deliberations in this way.

Now if we are convinced that Leibniz's determinism is true, we may well sit back and say to ourselves, "Why should I do anything? Everything is in God's hands, so I do not need to exert myself at all." But Leibniz has argued that if we do this, we shall be missing out on our highest happiness, which we experience as we see perfection in things. Yes, everything will turn out for the best – this Leibniz guarantees – but selfishly we should want to see the things in our lives turn out for the best, and so we should exert ourselves to help this to be the case. Consider: should we want it to be predetermined that we are slothful and in the midst of misery? Or should we want it to be predetermined that we act so as to bring about more happiness and perfection in the things around us? If it *seems* to us that we can bring about the latter, then it may well be that our endeavours – which, admittedly, are themselves predetermined – are just what is needed to determine the happy result.

Politics

It perhaps will come as no surprise that Leibniz favoured aristocracy. For one thing, his professional life was rooted in serving princes, princesses, queens and kings. But for another, he conceived the universe as a divine monarchy in which a wise and benevolent ruler made the soundest of all possible decrees. He held that individuals should try to do the same. And he held that communities should follow suit, under the leadership of wise and benevolent human beings. Like Plato, he felt no attraction towards democracy or republicanism, and could not see why anyone would want to be ruled by people who were not experts in justice.

Unfortunately, though, we often find our rulers to be something other than experts in justice. Still, even a tyrannical leader is typically capable of maintaining some form of civil order, even if it is not the best possible one. Leibniz seems to have followed Hobbes in preferring even unjust order to any kind of anarchy; and perhaps his experience with the Thirty Years War convinced him of this. But he disagreed with Hobbes about how humans would be in a state of nature. According to Hobbes, when effective government fails, people fall into "a war of all against all" – there is no real right and wrong without a government, and people will do whatever they want to do. But Leibniz, given his view of God and metaphysical perfectionism, believed that there is a real right and wrong, independent of any society, and he believed in natural obligations creatures have to one another. And he believed that humans, overall, have a natural inclination towards loving perfection wherever they find it, and they will form communities out of a concern for justice: it is not (as Hobbes maintained) merely a matter of pledging allegiance to a great big bully (the sovereign) out of fear of what others may do to you.

This point deserves further emphasis. Both Descartes and Spinoza built their moral and political theories on the basis of self-interest. For Descartes, it is in my own best interest to cultivate (what he termed) *generosity*. For Spinoza, self-interest was enough to lay the foundation for civic obligation, although that foundation must be supplemented either with (illusory) religious ideals or the dictates of reason. In Leibniz, though, there is a genuine love creatures have for one another, and a genuine interest they take in one another's perfection. We do not treat one another well *merely* out of self-interest (though self-interest plays some role). By nature, we are concerned for one another.

Leibniz also incorporated some fixtures of ancient Roman law into his political philosophy. According to the Romans, justice comes in three strengths. The lowest grade of justice is the precept to *injure no one* – so a minimally just society is one in which one may reasonably expect to be safe. The middle grade of justice is the precept was to *give each person his or her due*. That is, each person should get what he or she deserves. And the highest grade of justice is to *live honestly*, which Leibniz understood as living charitably, or loving others under the guidance of wisdom. Leibniz did not expect human societies to rise to the highest grade of justice; in such a perfect society, there would be no need for police or judges, there would be no private property, and all would be ruled by wisdom and love. It would be Eden, or heaven. But he did expect human societies to reach the middle grade of justice. Under a just government of this kind, we should expect that each citizen receives what he or she deserves. This requires both a sense of duty and benevolence. Following our duty means impartiality: we should expect that everyone is treated fairly by the law, and no one is treated as an exception. And in addition to this impartiality, Leibniz thinks that justice requires that the law be applied with *good will*, that is, with a genuine concern for one another's well-being: "The sense of the principle is this: do not do or do not refuse lightly that which you would not like to be done to you or which another would not refuse to you" (PW: 82).

Thus Leibnizian political justice aims beyond the goal of creating a society in which all can get along. Just "getting along" is not enough; justice requires that we actually care for one another and have an active interest in what each other deserve, and even an active interest in one another's happiness. Again, being just is a matter of emulating God, and trying to elicit perfection from fellow creatures, with any of the resources available to us. We strive to make this the best of all possible worlds, and in doing this we promote human happiness.

Promoting human happiness requires developing many of our distinctively human capacities:

> To contribute truly to the happiness of men, one must enlighten their understanding; one must fortify their will with the exercise of virtues, that is, in the habit of acting according to reason; and one must, finally, try to remove the obstacles which keep them from finding truth and following true goods.
> (PW: 105)

We may read this as advice about what a civil society must promote, if it is to perfect the middle grade of justice, and possibly work towards the highest grade of justice. "Giving each his due" means really understanding, in a full and thorough way, what each person's due truly is, and arranging society so that it may be delivered. As human beings, we are due understanding, good will, truth and true goods. A just society sees that we all obtain these things (or that we are justly refused them, if we have done something to deserve punishment).

Leibniz tried to convince the political leaders of his day that such a deep concern for justice was in fact in the rulers' own self-interest. To the extent that the rulers' subjects were wise, virtuous and happy, they would be more useful as subjects. And to the extent that subjects were occupied in pursuing virtue, they would be less likely to concern themselves with other things (gambling, drinking and fighting) that would bring about civil unrest. Leibniz also worked assiduously to convince both Catholics and Protestants that their doctrinal differences were not so serious as to make a reunion between the two unthinkable. He saw that a single Christian kingdom would stand a better chance of bringing about justice than two kingdoms at war with one another. And Leibniz also concerned himself with many particular political actions of the day with the aim of making his vision of justice become actual. Most of his advice, sadly, was ignored.

A political theodicy

For Leibniz, morality and justice are natural parts of the universe, as much as monads, forces and animalcules are. The universe itself is a just kingdom; and it is natural for human communities to try to emulate that kingdom, so far as it is possible:

> As for me, I put forward the great principle of metaphysics as well as of morality, that the world is governed by the most perfect intelligence which is possible, which means that one must consider it as a universal monarchy whose head is all-powerful and sovereignly wise, and whose subjects are all minds, that is, substances capable of relations or society with God; and that the rest is only the instrument of the glory of god and of the felicity of minds, and that as a result the entire universe is made for minds, such that it can contribute to their happiness as much as possible. (PW: 105)

The political structure of the universe is established with the aim of securing the greatest human happiness. Our human nature, which determines us to want this happiness, encourages us to set up our own political institutions accordingly. And so – according to our nature and the nature of the world – we shall want to establish societies that promote the greatest human flourishing. To do this requires wisdom, of course; and once we acknowledge this, Leibniz would believe that his own philosophical, political and metaphysical programme was already under way.

Key points

- Our fundamental moral obligation, according to Leibniz, is to love things in proportion to their degree of metaphysical perfection. This is justice, or "the charity of the wise".
- Our choices contribute in one way or another to this being the best of all possible worlds. Our choices are free to the extent that they arise from our own beliefs and desires, and to the extent that God could have created a different world in which other choices are made.
- Our political obligation is to create a society that promotes human perfection and human happiness.

Conclusion

Is rationalism plausible?

Rationalism is founded on an extraordinary assumption: that human reason has within itself the resources for discerning and understanding reality's deepest fixtures. It is easy to imagine this assumption being false. Perhaps human reason is simply incapable of working out the deepest truths about reality, or perhaps we can do so only through extensive empirical investigation. Perhaps human reason evolved under prehistoric pressures, and we are very talented at building fires and catching rabbits but very poor at doing metaphysics. Perhaps there is no such thing as ultimate reality, as crazy at that may sound, and all human experience is nothing but interpretations upon interpretations. Perhaps the biggest truths are inconceivable. All of these are possibilities, but rationalism denies them. As said in the introduction, rationalism holds that the innermost skeleton of reality and the innermost skeleton of the human mind are one and the same.

And what do our rationalists conclude? Descartes concludes that there are two radically different kinds of substance in the world, minds and bodies, and that in every person there is one of each in mysterious interaction. Spinoza concludes that there can be only one substance, which is both thinking and extended, and that the apparent individuals in the universe are in fact particular ways in which that one substance is expressed. Leibniz concludes that there are infinitely many minds which mirror one another in such a way as to produce the appearance of a shared world of bodies in motion. These conclusions differ so radically from one another that one may be excused for wondering how mind and reality could possibly share a skeleton, if no two rationalists' minds share one!

David Hume (1711–76) was very sceptical of the rationalists' assumption, and wrote that the metaphysics of the most profound and abstract philosophies

> arise either from the fruitless efforts of human vanity, which tries to penetrate into subjects utterly inaccessible to the understanding, or from the craft of popular superstitions, which, being unable to defend themselves on fair ground, raise these entangling brambles to cover and protect their weakness.
> (*Enquiry*: §1)

So, in other words, the great metaphysicians are either proudly sailing out of their depth, or shamefully hiding themselves behind confusing tangles of metaphysical propositions. Either way, they are not coming clean and admitting that they just do not know. It is easy for this to happen when a philosopher chains his mind to metaphysical principles and their logical consequences. Hume again:

> It is easy for a profound philosopher to commit a mistake in his subtle reasonings; and one mistake is the necessary parent of another, while he pushes on his consequences, and is not deterred from embracing any conclusion, by its unusual appearance, or its contradiction to popular opinion. (*Ibid.*)

Many philosophers have shared Hume's conclusion that the great metaphysical systems of the rationalists are nothing more than the dreams of geniuses who mistook their own creations for what necessarily must be the case.

Yet, for all that, there is a powerful attraction to rationalism. How are we to discover what *must* be true, except by consulting our own conceptual powers? Nature does not show us any necessity – it shows only what *happens* to be true. If we are ever to discern an ultimate set of fixtures that limit what can happen and what can come about, we have only our reason to trust. And what human being can resist the desire to know?

Kant

Immanuel Kant (1724–1804) recognized that human beings are saddled with questions they can neither answer nor ignore. The great questions confronted by the rationalists – What is ultimately real? What are the origins of the world? What is consciousness? – are questions human beings must raise, just by virtue of being intelligent agents. To understand anything, we must ask *why*; and nothing stops us from extending our *whys* to the deepest and most puzzling facets of our experience. But at the same time, Kant said, we are unable to establish any answers to these questions, and a close study of the rationalists could be said to prove his point. The rationalists' arguments are seldom based on clear and obvious mistakes in logic, or when they are, there is usually a way to repair the flaw. Some of the assumptions they make are strange to our minds (such as the gradations of reality thesis). But clearly the assumptions seemed to them to be unexceptionable, and we can still see some plausibility in them, after sufficient reflection. Overall, each rationalist employed his reason with intelligence and good judgement. But they came to such very different conclusions. Kant inferred from this that human reason simply does not have the competence to secure metaphysical conclusions, despite our infallible inclination to try to do so. And he used this conclusion to leverage some metaphysics of his own.

If human reason really is incapable of coming to know metaphysical truth, then there must be some explanation for its rather amazing competence when it comes to knowing natural truth. The rationalists and Kant all lived in eras when modern science was advancing rapidly, and Newtonian physics promised to unlock all the secrets of the natural world. It was clear to the philosophers that human reason certainly does have the competence to understand nature. Why then should it be competent to know nature, but not competent to know nature's foundations? Why is it that the human mind can grasp the most universal truths of mathematics, and the most fundamental laws of nature, but not the nature of substance, or causality, or mind? Kant's answer was to turn this puzzle into a declaration: the human mind can know anything within the boundaries of nature, that is, within the boundaries of human experience, but it can know nothing beyond those borders. And why is this? Because, Kant suggested, the boundaries of human experience are the boundaries of the human mind, but these boundaries do not coincide with the boundaries of metaphysical reality. In other words, there is some truth in rationalism: the skeleton of what humans can possibly experience and the skeleton of the human mind are one and the same. The world we can experience has the same shape and limitations as what we can or cannot conceive. But when it comes to what we cannot possibly experience – the universe in its entirety, the whole of time, the immaterial soul – then all bets are off. There is no guarantee of any correspondence whatsoever between mind and reality. Here scepticism triumphs.

The rationalists' problem, Kant thought, was that they tried to apply human reason beyond the bounds of its applicability. As a result, they were able to "prove" too many things, since their arguments ran unchecked by the bounds of possible human experience. The lesson to be learned is that human beings should continue to explore and understand their own experience, but cease to insist upon dogmatic answers to metaphysical questions. We can be realists about science, but sceptics about metaphysics and religion. (Well, in fact Kant believed that there are many religious beliefs we ought to maintain, if only to encourage moral behaviour. But the basis of religion, he contended, was faith, not knowledge.)

German idealism

But several other philosophers found that Kant's conclusion left too many questions dangling. Why should it be that human experience and the human mind share the same structure? What explanation is there for that coincidence? And what is the human mind anyway? It seems as if it can neither be an object within human experience nor an object outside it. For if it lies within human experience, it cannot be responsible for determining the limits of human experience. On the other hand, if it lies outside human experience, then why should it be at all limited by human experience? Without securing answers to these questions, these philosophers felt, we are left with nothing but scepticism. For what reason would we have to think that the human mind and human experience would necessarily share the same structure?

Just as philosophers were raising these questions, there arose a debate between F. H. Jacobi (1743–1819) and Moses Mendelssohn (1729–86). The debate was over whether a third philosopher, the great G. E. Lessing (1729–81), had been a *Spinozist*. The controversy became quite a battle, with many different voices chiming in with different arguments to offer, but the controversy was not just over Lessing.

It was over the nature and scope of philosophical reason. To be a Spinozist is to believe that all reality originates from a single, unified and knowable source. Those philosophers who wanted to tie up Kant's loose ends into a comprehensive theory that explained everything would be advancing a kind of Spinozism. And we all know that advancing Spinozism means advancing determinism, necessitarianism and eventually atheism. Those philosophers who did not believe Kant's loose ends could be tied neatly into an explain-it-all system were left grounding their beliefs in some kind of faith, which would prove that philosophical knowledge is always subordinate to faith. The Spinoza controversy (or "*Pantheismusstreit*"), as it came to be known, stemmed from a very sharp difference in attitude towards philosophy's power. Some believed it was possible for philosophy to fit everything into a rational system, while others believed that there are truths – especially religious truths – that reason can never comprehend. Each philosopher felt he must choose: be a Spinozist, or be a theist.

The German idealists after Kant were all wrestling with the promise and threat of rationalism. A philosopher's job, it could be said, is to find the unity in all domains of knowledge: to render thought and being one and the same. But there is a powerful pull within revealed religions towards believing that not everything can be unified, at least not by any creature's mind. To fit God into a rational system is to deny God, and to affirm the transcendent God is to deny reason's final authority. One might see the battlefield of German idealism as an intellectual war fought over rationalism. Two of the great warriors left standing at the end were G. W. F. Hegel (1770–1831), who tried to fold religion into reason, and Søren Kierkegaard (1813–55), who believed that Christianity must ultimately renounce reason.

The Enlightenment

Spinoza did not merely inspire the Spinoza controversy. His *Theological-Political Treatise* also forced later philosophers to examine the relations among religious authority, the state and an individual's own rationality. Human beings, at least in principle, are able to cultivate their own reason and perform experiments and put forward both a science of the natural world and a science of human history. When they do so, it is hard to avoid Spinoza's conclusion that the Bible should be seen as a compilation of ancient texts whose authors were neither natural scientists nor historians. The Bible cannot be taken as literally true, if we are to be consistent with the conclusions science and history would have us draw. Religions based upon the Bible may be useful in getting less rational people to behave in virtuous ways, but these religions cannot be seen as providing much more than that. This raises a political challenge: how do we establish a society that allows for such religions, or even employs their services, while at the same time carving out a free space for philosophy, science and history to grow? This is the problem of *political toleration*, and it is at the centre of a movement of thought known as the *Enlightenment*.

The Enlightenment was a multidimensional revolution in thought, occurring in art, literature, philosophy, science and politics. Kant wrote an essay suggesting that its motto should be "Dare to use your own reason!" Indeed, the central thrust of the Enlightenment was to trust in the latent abilities in human beings to secure their own past, present and future. Humans do not need special authorities to discern their own history, or establish civil order, or to see what the future will bring. Priests and kings, in the end, are like any of us, with no special access to the truth. So the Enlightenment was deeply anti-authority in temperament. And Spinoza was seen as an emblem of the Enlightenment, both because of his published conclusions and because of his anti-authoritarian temperament. Indeed, the promise of rationalism was inherent in the Enlightenment's hopes. We can dare to use our own reason only if we believe we have this reason, and we believe that it can deliver important truths that stand on their own, apart from the many biased and prejudiced ways in which we have been brought up.

But alas, many theories and programmes brought forward under the banner of the Enlightenment show as much bias and prejudice as they do rationality, and this has led many to wonder whether we really should dare to use our own reason. Our own reason has brought us industrialization as well as the capability of waging horrific world wars, to say nothing of fascistic regimes and genocides. Perhaps rationalism and the Enlightenment are nothing more than biases and prejudices of a privileged class of people, anxious to find not rationality but *rationalizations* for their ways of life. It may be noted that Descartes, Spinoza and Leibniz may have had high estimations about the basic human ability to reason, but what this really came down to was a high opinion of each human's capacity to be a good European. Scholars are still arguing whether this is a case in which the rationalists simply did not follow their reason all the way through, or whether it is indicative of a problem inherent to rationalism.

Partial successes

Rationalism remains today a cogent philosophical response to at least three important problematic subject areas. First, there is the question of exactly how humans gain their language abilities. Noam Chomsky revolutionized the field of linguistics by positing structures innate in the human mind which are responsible for helping speakers to gain and use a language. (One of his early books was in fact entitled *Cartesian Linguistics*.) It is safe to say that linguists generally agree with something like Leibniz's "veined marble" analogy, believing that the human mind is predisposed towards certain grammatical structures. Second, there is the question of how claims made about the world have *meaning*. Some philosophers believe that an adequate account of meaning must employ concepts and propositions that exist independently of particular mental events and concepts held by individual thinkers. They think these concepts and propositions must be treated as purely conceptual objects, somewhat like Plato's forms. Finally, some philosophers also believe that certain metaphysical problems (such as the problem of causation) can be solved only by positing *a priori* metaphysical knowledge in human beings. All these thinkers believe that there are some elements of human knowledge or experience that simply cannot be "naturalized", since they play roles that are deeper or more foundational than anything that can be learned naturally. So rationalism remains a "live approach" to several contemporary problems.

If we set aside these reflections about rationalism as a broad enterprise, and look more particularly at some of the claims made by Descartes, Spinoza and Leibniz, we can appreciate several significant philosophical claims each of them made which we would today regard as on the right track or even exactly right.

Although most philosophers today deny Descartes's dualism, two things should be said in its favour. First, Descartes did articulate a view of the mind and body that many have found to be especially intuitive, at least in a "pre-philosophical" sense. Consciousness does seem like a feature only a mind can have. It is hard to imagine a purely physical entity, even a complex one, somehow being vividly aware of itself and its environment. The dimension of awareness is an *inner* one, inescapably, and not public in the way that the workings of machines are. One can study a brain to any degree of detail and still not know *what thinking is going on in there*, it seems. So it must be admitted that, even if we finally reject Descartes's theory, there is something initially compelling about it. Second, as Descartes tried to explain the workings of the body and brain, he adopted the right strategy. He knew nothing of electricity, or biochemistry, so his account failed. But the strategy of explaining bodily behaviour as one would explain the workings of a machine proved to be sound. It is just that there are some physical forces he did not know about.

Many contemporary thinkers have found even more promise in aspects of Spinoza's philosophy. Spinoza tried to integrate mind and body, in a way, and tie mental states to physical states. He also recognized that the emotions and reason cannot always be neatly separated, and that what we feel is always bound up with what we think. His programme for dealing with harmful emotions – as well as Descartes's – can be seen as a predecessor of several clinical psychologies being used today. His political work is read alongside Hobbes's and Locke's as being of fundamental importance in understanding modern political thought. And his research into the Bible is still read today as one of the earliest works in modern biblical criticism.

Leibniz's philosophy has also had some success, by contemporary lights. His understanding of space as a set of relations, rather than as a stand-alone container for bodies in motion, was taken very seriously by philosophers and physicists at least until the theoretical advances made by Einstein. Now it is hard to say to what extent he got it right, since Einstein changed so many basic assumptions, but it does seem clear that space, or spacetime, is closer to what he imagined than to any other competing theory. His contributions in mathematics and logic are as solid as ever, and when students today employ calculus, they use his system. And Leibniz's theology is still of interest to philosophical theologians today, especially on the difficult matter of reconciling human freedom with God's omnipotence.

Thus, despite many criticisms that can be raised against their philosophical systems as a whole, the rationalists got many important things right, as near as we can tell. Any general argument against their philosophical stance must take into account not only their shortcomings, but these successes as well.

Questions for discussion and revision

one Descartes's dualistic world

1. Why does Descartes think that, for all he knows, he could be dreaming? Would he not have to know what waking life is in order to know what a dream is?
2. Given Descartes's physics, how do you suppose he would account for the difference between light and darkness?
3. What reasons does Descartes have for thinking mind and body are distinct substances? Why not think of the mind as somehow produced by the functioning of the brain?
4. Descartes proves God's existence, and that God is no deceiver; thus he can trust that what he clearly and distinctly perceives is true. But if he doubts what he clearly and distinctly perceives, how can he trust his own argument that God exists?
5. If God creates our intellects to have the structure they have, then is it not possible that – for some good reason – God fashioned our intellects to give us wrong answers sometimes? What might Descartes say to this objection?

two Descartes's morals and *The Passions of the Soul*

1. How would you describe the attitude I should take towards my society, according to Descartes?
2. What kind of happiness can non-human animals feel, according to Descartes, given that they have no soul? What kind of happiness *can they not* feel?
3. Compare the happiness you feel when you have acted with great self-control with the happiness you feel when something lucky comes your way. Which happiness is better? Why?

4. "Descartes simply uses the word 'perfection' for the sorts of qualities he likes. In nature nothing is 'more perfect' than anything else." How might Descartes reply to this objection?
5. What sorts of things might prevent someone from gaining *generosity*, as Descartes calls it? Might some people be completely incapable of it?

three Spinoza's one substance

1. Descartes believed that distinct minds can share an attribute (thought), but Spinoza denied that substances can share attributes. How might Spinoza argue in order to persuade Descartes to change his mind?
2. What makes an idea inadequate, according to Spinoza?
3. Spinoza has been called a "pantheist", which is someone who believes that everything is God. Is this an accurate description of his view? Would he say that his left shoe is identical with God?
4. One of the earliest objections to Spinoza's philosophy was this: "If everything is in some sense identical with God, then that means everything humans do (wage war, murder, etc.) is really done by God. But God would never do such things!" How might Spinoza reply to this objection?
5. Spinoza thinks knowledge of the first kind (through imagination and casual experience) is always inadequate. Does this mean everything that we can know can be demonstrated? If so, does this seem plausible?

four Spinoza's ethics, politics and religion

1. According to Spinoza, our essence is a striving to continue to exist. Why then do people do things that bring harm to themselves?
2. Would the "free man" experience any emotions or passions?
3. Suppose I could steal a doughnut without any fear of getting caught. Should I do so, according to Spinoza? Why or why not?
4. Since humans are almost always at the mercy of their emotions, why would Spinoza advocate democracy? Would he not think of it as a kind of rule by the mob? What advantages does democracy have?
5. If Spinoza thinks religion is an effective tool for keeping less rational people in line, why would he publish a book which exposes the Bible as being fundamentally wrong about many things?

five Leibniz's world of monads

1. Suppose you and I are looking at the same tree. What would "the same tree" mean in Leibniz's metaphysics? In what sense would we be viewing the *same* object?
2. According to Leibniz, what makes your body *your* body, instead of mine?

3. Leibniz believed that the universe is governed by laws of nature. But at the same time he denied the fundamental reality of bodies. How then would he explain the truth of the laws of physics?
4. There are some things I can know only by experience (such as, for example, the height of the tallest living giraffe). But Leibniz thinks all statements are analytically true. Why then cannot I know everything merely by reflecting on the meanings of words?
5. Suppose God allows a miracle to occur (like the parting of the Red Sea). What would God have to do, metaphysically, for such an event to occur? And why would it count as a *miracle*?

six Leibniz's justice and freedom

1. Leibniz thinks it has been analytically true, since the beginning of the world, that you would be reading this now. In what sense then could you have *avoided* reading this now?
2. According to Leibniz, what makes one choice better than another?
3. Why, according to Leibniz, are we motivated to have concern for one another?
4. Would Leibniz think we are ever justified in lying, if it seems to us that doing so would bring about a greater good?
5. What would be the just way of dealing with criminals, according to Leibniz? What would be our aim in punishing them?

Further reading

Full references for these books can be found in the bibliography.

Beginning level

Oxford University Press's *Spinoza: A Very Short Introduction* by Roger Scruton and *Descartes: A Very Short Introduction* by Tom Sorell offer short – very short! – and accurate overviews of the philosophers' lives and thoughts. (As of this writing, there is no such introduction to Leibniz, unfortunately.) Matthew Stewart's *The Courtier and the Heretic* is an engaging account of the lives of Spinoza and Leibniz, and the tense relationships between their views of the world. Garrett Thomson, in *Bacon to Kant: An Introduction to Modern Philosophy*, provides a quick and clear account of the rationalists' thoughts (along with others').

Intermediate level

The Stanford Encyclopedia of Philosophy, edited by Edward Zalta, provides excellent overviews and discussions of the lives and philosophies of Descartes, Spinoza and Leibniz. It is available online at http://plato.stanford.edu. Each article also offers helpful bibliographies. John Cottingham's *The Rationalists* provides a thematic discussion of the rationalists' thought, with chapters exploring the relations among the philosophers' conclusions about substance, mind, freedom and so on. There are also excellent books on each of the philosophers, suitable for readers with a solid but not specialized knowledge of philosophy: John Cottingham's *Descartes*, Henry Allison's *Benedict de Spinoza: An Introduction*, and Nicholas Jolley's *Leibniz*.

Advanced level

Jonathan Bennett's two-volume work, *Learning from Six Philosophers*, is an excellent source for uncovering the deep philosophical problems each philosopher faces. It is written in sharp and elegant prose. Most of the treatment of the rationalists is to be found in the first volume. There are many good works that examine what two or more of the philosophers thought about this or that topic, but here are two well worth exploring: Nicholas Jolley's *The Light of the Soul: Theories of Ideas in Leibniz, Malebranche, and Descartes*, and Roger Woolhouse's *Descartes, Spinoza, and Leibniz: The Concept of Substance in Seventeenth Century Metaphysics*. Along these lines – and also as the classical work decrying the traditional rationalist/empiricist distinction – is Louis Loeb's *From Descartes to Hume: Continental Metaphysics and the Development of Modern Philosophy*. And there are many excellent books dedicated to each philosopher. Here are some recommendations. For Descartes, Margaret Wilson's *Descartes*. For Spinoza, Edwin Curley's *Behind the Geometrical Method* and Alan Donagan's *Spinoza*. For Leibniz, Robert Adams's *Leibniz: Determinist, Theist, Idealist* and Stuart Brown's *Leibniz*. For the influence of the rationalists (especially Spinoza) on the Enlightenment, one should read Jonathan Israel's *Radical Enlightenment*. These books are written for specialists, or for students in philosophy well beyond the intermediate level.

Bibliography

Quotations (and summaries) in the text are drawn from these sources:

Primary sources

Berkeley, George. 1998. *A Treatise Concerning the Principles of Human Knowledge.* Edited by Jonathan Dancy. Oxford: Oxford University Press.

Descartes, René. 1964–74. *Oeuvres de Descartes*, 11 vols. Edited by C. Adam and P. Tannery. Paris: CNRS/Vrin.

Descartes, René. 1985. *The Philosophical Writings of Descartes*, 3 vols. Translated by John Cottingham, Robert Stoothoff, Dugald Murdoch and Anthony Kenny. Cambridge: Cambridge University Press. (Includes *Discourse on Method, Meditations on First Philosophy, Principles of Philosophy* and other works.)

Descartes, René. 1989. *The Passions of the Soul.* Translated by Stephen H. Voss. Indianapolis, IN: Hackett.

Hobbes, Thomas. 1994. *Leviathan.* Edited by Edwin Curley. Indianapolis, IN: Hackett.

Hume, D. 1993. *An Enquiry Concerning Human Understanding.* Edited by Eric Steinberg. Indianapolis, IN: Hackett.

Leibniz, G. W. 1988. *Political Writings.* Translated and edited by Patrick Riley. Second edition. Cambridge: Cambridge University Press.

Leibniz, G. W. 1989. *Philosophical Essays.* Translated by Roger Ariew and Daniel Garber. Indianapolis, IN: Hackett. (Includes *Discourse on Metaphysics, Monadology, On Ultimate Origination of Things* and other works.)

Leibniz, G. W. 1996. *New Essays on Human Understanding.* Translated and edited by Peter Remnant and Jonathan Bennett. Cambridge: Cambridge University Press.

Locke, John. 1959. *An Essay concerning Human Understanding.* 2 vols. New York: Dover.
Plato. 1997. *Plato: Complete Works.* Edited by John M. Cooper. Indianapolis, IN: Hackett. (Includes *Phaedo.*)
Spinoza, B. 1985. *The Collected Works of Spinoza.* Translated and edited by Edwin Curley. First vol. Princeton, NJ: Princeton University Press. (Includes *Ethics* and *Treatise on the Emendation of the Intellect.*)
Spinoza, B. 1998. *Theological-Political Treatise.* Translated by Samuel Shirley. Indianapolis, IN: Hackett.
Spinoza, B. 2000. *Political Treatise.* Translated by Samuel Shirley. Indianapolis, IN: Hackett.

Secondary sources

Adams, Robert. 1994. *Leibniz: Determinist, Theist, Idealist.* Oxford: Oxford University Press.
Allison, Henry. 1987. *Benedict de Spinoza: An Introduction.* New Haven, CT: Yale University Press.
Bennett, Jonathan. 1984. *A Study of Spinoza's* Ethics. Indianapolis, IN: Hackett.
Bennett, Jonathan. 2001. *Learning from Six Philosophers.* 2 vols. Oxford: Oxford University Press.
Brown, Stuart. 1984. *Leibniz.* Brighton: Harvester.
Cottingham, John. 1986. *Descartes.* Oxford: Blackwell.
Cottingham, John. 1988. *The Rationalists.* Oxford: Oxford University Press.
Cottingham, John (ed.). 1992. *The Cambridge Companion to Descartes.* Cambridge: Cambridge University Press.
Curley, Edwin. 1987. *Behind the Geometrical Method.* Princeton, NJ: Princeton University Press.
Donagan, Alan. *Spinoza.* Chicago, IL: University of Chicago Press.
Garber, Daniel. 1992. *Descartes' Metaphysical Physics.* Chicago, IL: University of Chicago Press.
Garber, Daniel. 2001. *Descartes Embodied.* Cambridge: Cambridge University Press.
Garrett, Don (ed.). 1996. *The Cambridge Companion to Spinoza.* Cambridge: Cambridge University Press.
Hampshire, Stuart. 1951. *Spinoza.* New York: Penguin.
Hatfield, Gary. 2002. *Descartes and the Meditations (Routledge Philosophy GuideBooks).* London: Routledge.
Henrich, Dieter. 2003. *Between Kant and Hegel: Lectures on German Idealism.* Edited by David S. Pacini. Cambridge, MA: Harvard University Press.
Israel, Jonathan. 2001. *Radical Enlightenment: Philosophy and the Making of Modernity 1650–1750.* Oxford: Oxford University Press.
Jolley, Nicholas. 1990. *The Light of the Soul: Theories of Ideas in Leibniz, Malebranche, and Descartes.* Oxford: Oxford University Press.
Jolley, Nicholas. 2005. *Leibniz.* London: Routledge.

Jolley, Nicholas (ed.). 1995. *The Cambridge Companion to Leibniz*. Cambridge: Cambridge University Press.

Loeb, Louis E. 1981. *From Descartes to Hume: Continental Metaphysics and the Development of Modern Philosophy*. Ithaca, NY: Cornell University Press.

Nadler, Steven. 1999. *Spinoza: A Life*. Cambridge: Cambridge University Press.

Phemister, Pauline. 2006. *The Rationalists: Descartes, Spinoza and Leibniz*. Cambridge: Polity.

Rutherford, Donald. 1995. *Leibniz and the Rational Order of Nature*. Cambridge: Cambridge University Press.

Rutherford, Donald, "Descartes' Ethics", *The Stanford Encyclopedia of Philosophy (Fall 2003 Edition)*, Edward N. Zalta (ed.). URL: http://plato.stanford.edu/archives/fall2003/entries/descartes-ethics/>.

Scruton, Roger. 2002. *Spinoza: A Very Short Introduction*. Oxford: Oxford University Press.

Sorell, Tom. 2001. *Descartes: A Very Short Introduction*. Oxford: Oxford University Press.

Stewart, Matthew. 2006. *The Courtier and the Heretic*. New York: Norton.

Thomson, Garrett. 2002. *Bacon to Kant: An Introduction to Modern Philosophy*. Prospect Heights, IL: Waveland Press.

Watson, Richard. 2002. *Cogito ergo sum: The Life of Rene Descartes*. Boston, MA: David R. Godine.

Wilson, Margaret. 1978. *Descartes*. London: Routledge.

Woolhouse, Roger. 1993. *Descartes, Spinoza, and Leibniz: The Concept of Substance in Seventeenth Century Metaphysics*. London: Routledge.

Youpa, Andrew, "Leibniz's Ethics", *The Stanford Encyclopedia of Philosophy (Winter 2004 Edition)*, Edward N. Zalta (ed.), URL: <http://plato.stanford.edu/archives/win2004/entries/leibniz-ethics/>.

Index

Aquinas 58, 109
Aristotle 25

Berkeley, George 113
bodies 31–3, 76–8, 112–16

Chomsky, Noam 153
conatus 86

Descartes
 on animals 38
 biography 17–18
 on Christianity 14–15
 on the *cogito* 22–3
 on doubting 20–21
 on God 23–5
 on the intellect 6–7
 Meditations 19–20
 on mind–body problem 38–40
 on morals 41–5
 on passions 54–7
 on politics 13
 on provisional moral code 41–5
 on religion 58–9
determinism 78–80, 85–7, 89–91, 137–41
dualism 29–31

Elisabeth, Princess of Bohemia 39, 42–3, 46
Enlightenment 151–2
extension 76–8

freedom of the will 37, 54–5, 78–9, 86–9, 137–8, 140–41

Galileo 18, 44
generosity 51, 53
God 10–11, 24–5, 69–70, 99–102
gradations of reality thesis 9–10, 49–50, 66, 130–32

happiness 46–8, 102–4
Hegel, G. W. F. 151
Hobbes, Thomas 88, 143
Hume, David 148
hylomorphism 34–5
hylozoism 118–19

individuation
 of bodies 32–3, 77
 of minds 36
innate ideas 4–5, 23, 27–8, 80–81
intellect *versus* imagination 6–7, 26–7

Jacobi, F. H. 150

Kant, Immanuel 92, 149–50
Kierkegaard, S. 151

Leeuwenhoek, Anton van 118–19
Leibniz
  biography 107–9
  on Christianity 15
  on complete concepts 120–22
  on determinism 112–17, 137–41
  on God 126–7
  on innate ideas 5
  metaphysics, basic picture 110–12
  on mind–body problem 116–17, 119–20
  on morals 13, 132–6
  on organisms 118–19
  philosophical temperament 109–10
  on the physical world 112–14, 117
  on politics 14, 142–6
  on substances 115–16
  on truth 120–22
Lessing, G. E. 150
Locke, John 4–5

Mendelssohn, M. 150
Minds 36, 38
mind–body problem 38–40, 70–72, 85–7, 116–17, 119–20
morals 12–13, 91–5, 132–6
motion 33–4

natural light 22–3, 81–2
necessitarianism 73–5, 122–6
Nietzsche, Friedrich 89

occasionalism 33, 38, 116

panpsychism 71–2
Pantheismusstreit 150–51
Plato 8, 90
politics 13–14, 95–9, 101–2, 142–6
principle of sufficient reason 23–4

rationalism
  contrasted with empiricism 1–2
  plausibility of 147–9
  success of 153–4
  rationalist epistemology 2–8
  rationalist metaphysics 8–12
reason 48–9
  dictates of 51–3, 93–5
religion 14–15, 96, 99–102, 151–2

soul 11–12, 104–6
Spinoza
  biography 61–2
  on Christianity 15, 99–102
  determinism 78–80
  on eternity of the mind 104–6
  on extension 76–8
  on the free man 87–9
  on freedom of speech 101–2
  geometrical method 63–4
  on knowledge 80–2
  on mind–body problem 70–72, 85–7
  on modes 67–9
  on morals 12–13, 91–5
  on passions 89–90
  on politics 14, 95–9, 101–2
  on psychotherapy 102–4
  on religion 62, 69–70
  on the sage 95–7
  on substances 64–6
Spinoza controversy (among German idealists) 150–51
Stoicism 12–13
substance monism 64–6

unactualized possibles 73–4, 80, 110, 138–40
universal harmony 116–17

vacuum 31, 76
virtue 50–51
Voltaire, F-M, A. 129

will 37